Collins
MUSIC

DELIVERING THE EY...

EARLY YEARS FOUNDATION STAGE

AGES 3-5

playing
learning
teaching

observation · assessment
practitioner · child · planning
environment · parents

BOOK SOLD
NO LONGER R.H.P.L.
PROPERTY

SUE NICHOLLS AND
SALLY HICKMAN

INTRODUCTION

The *Early Years Foundation Stage (EYFS) statutory framework* introduced in September 2021 recognises that every child deserves the best possible start in life to help them to thrive. This resource has been written to support the delivery of this revised framework and to help support dedicated practitioners to provide activities, opportunities and scaffolding to ensure children develop and make progress in their learning through the educational programmes of the EYFS.

This book forms part of the *Music Express* series and musical learning is an intrinsic part of the holistic EYFS provision provided in this resource. Original songs and chants and new lyrics sung to traditional melodies forge strong links with the theme of each starting point, and carefully selected pieces of recorded music develop listening skills. Children's creative responses are encouraged through singing, playing, movement and dance. (For more musical support, see online resources.)

The child's voice

The 12 'starting points' in this resource were selected in Early Years settings through working with and listening to children exploring their current interests, and we hope your children will enjoy both the adult-guided activities and the opportunities to engage and direct their own play and learning.

The image and short introduction for each starting point are intended to prompt your own discussion with children, to listen to them and establish their level of understanding of the subject area. Through effective questioning and debate, this will allow you to delve more deeply into children's knowledge and understanding, helping to guide and tailor the delivery of the curriculum to challenge and extend children's skills and knowledge to a much greater depth.

Scaffolding

We value 'continuous provision' as a key element of high-quality early years practice and have included ideas and enhancements to excite, engage and motivate children in their chosen play, both indoors and outdoors. With adult support and effective high-quality interactions, practitioners can spontaneously scaffold children's development and learning.

The activities are planned for children between the ages of three to five. However, some of the continuous provision could be slightly adapted and amended to support the learning and development of children under three.

Every child is unique

Every child will have experienced many differences in their young lives from family and community diversity, cultural and religious experience and access to the many different forms of educational, health and social care support. Some children will need a little extra help to access the curriculum, but with the right support all children will thrive and make progress.

Our aim is to be totally inclusive and some activities may need to be adapted and amended to ensure that all children wishing to take part are able to do so as independently as possible.

Balanced learning

We provide activities to support adult-guided learning covering the developmental programmes for ages 3–4 and 4–5 across all seven areas of learning and development in the EYFS (Communication and Language; Personal, Social and Emotional Development; Physical Development; Literacy; Mathematics; Understanding the World; Expressive Arts and Design). The areas of Communication and Language and Literacy are linked to phase one of 'Letters and sounds' and will, hopefully, lay a secure foundation to underpin your chosen phonics scheme at the appropriate developmental stage to help children progress.

It is important to give children the appropriate balance of adult-guided learning with opportunities for children to lead their own learning that is appropriate for their age and stage of development.

It is always worth remembering that young children are only able to remain totally focussed and concentrate for short periods of time, usually for the minutes of their age plus one minute. However, when leading their own play and learning children can become fully engaged and remain focussed for much longer periods.

Observation, assessment and planning

To enable a child to grow and blossom, they need equal measures of playing, learning and teaching, supported by parents, practitioners and their environments, with observation, assessment and planning underpinning this high-quality early years practice. (For more information about the observation, assessment and planning cycle, see online resources).

Supporting resources

The accompanying CD includes the narrated stories, listening pieces and performances of the original songs and new songs sung to traditional melodies, composed for this resource. These are also included in the online resources along with backing tracks for the original songs, other supporting resources and activities to support 'home learning' to accompany each individual starting point. There is also an overview document online, which provides musical support and a description of the observation, assessment, planning cycle.

See **collins.co.uk/CPMEYFS/download**

Contents and CD track list

Introduction	2
Contents and CD track list	**3**

Starting points
Developed from the children's interests

Who shall I be today? — 4

- 1 Story: *Let's find treasure*
- 2 Song: *Dressing up* (alternative verses CD track 3)
- 4 Song: *Being someone new*

Let's go green! — 8

- 5 Song: *Recycled robot*
- 6 Song: *Let's recycle!*
- 7 Listening: Stephen Chadwick – *Concerto for robotic piano and strings*

Busy city — 12

- 8 Song: *Living in the city*
- 9 Rap: *Crazy city*
- 10 Listening: Dmitry Kabalevsky – *Galop*

Beyond the stars — 16

- 11 Story: *Zigi bounces to Mars*
- 12 Song: *Space hopper take me to Mars*
- 13 Song: *Rocket ride*
- 14 Listening: George Crumb – *Music of the starry night* (extract)

When snowflakes fall — 20

- 15 Poem: *My snowman*
- 16 Song: *Snowflakes fall*
- 17 Song: *Jack Frost's fingers*
- 18 Listening: Franz Liszt – *La campanella* (extract)

Fabulous food — 24

- 19 Story: *Ai Lin cooks chow mein*
- 20 Song: *Yummy, yummy yum cha*
- 21 Song: *Noodle song*

A tale from long ago — 28

- 22 Story: *The helpful elves*
- 23 Song: *The shoemaker's piggy bank*
- 24 Chant: *One pair of shoes*
- 25 Song: *Midnight*
- 26 Song: *Presents for the elves*
- 27 Listening: Jennifer Higdon – *Impressions: III. To the point* (extract)

Our growing world — 32

- 28 Song: *Sunflower seeds*
- 29 Song: *Growing up!*

Do you see dinosaurs? — 36

- 30 Poem: *Tyro the baby dinosaur*
- 31 Song: *Dinosaur parade*
- 32 Song: *Tyrannosaurus rex*
- 33 Listening: Sergei Prokofiev – *Dance of the knights* (extract)

A sky full of colour — 40

- 34 Story: *Danny's tasty rainbow*
- 35 Song: *Colours shining*
- 36 Song: *Look out for rainbows*
- 37 Listening: Toru Takemitsu – *Ame no ki (Rain tree)* (extract)

Amazing African animals — 44

- 38 Story: *Searching in the Serengeti*
- 39 Song: *Mangwane mpulele*
- 40 Song: *Come to the Serengeti*

Under the sea — 48

- 41 Story: *Seashells for Serena*
- 42 Song: *Sea creatures*
- 43 Song: *The sea is stuck in a shell*
- 44 Listening: Camille Saint-Saëns – *Aquarium*

Stories and poems	**52**
Acknowledgements	**56**

WHO SHALL I BE TODAY?

Young children love to dress up and pretend to be someone else. Through imaginative play they can act out their hopes and dreams, practise their emotions, imitate a character and develop their communication and language skills. The actions involved in putting on costumes will also develop the physical skills of dressing and undressing independently.

Print out the image (see online resources) and stick it onto card to create a message label that says 'Who will you be today?'. Attach this to a basket or suitcase filled with dressing-up clothes for the children to explore, and tie it up with a large and enticing bow. (Be mindful that the subject matter of pirates, boats and water may be triggering for some children and adapt as necessary.)

ENHANCING CONTINUOUS PROVISION

Play dough
Provide jewels and confetti for children to add to play dough to create their own treasures. Help children to make a treasure chest in which to store all their newly-created sparkly items.

Water
Add mild detergent or baby shampoo to the water tray and encourage children to wash clothing items from the role play area. Have another bowl of water ready for rinsing. Hang up a washing line in the outdoor area and provide pegs so that children can hang the wet clothes out to dry.

Sand
Let the sand tray become a place of buried treasure, e.g. spray stones with gold, silver and metallic paints, bury strings of beads and chains (sourced from charity shops) and add any plastic tiaras, jewels and gold coins that you may have in your environment already.

Small world and construction
Ask children to create scenes involving their favourite characters and encourage them to inhabit those imagined worlds in their play. Provide small-world and construction toys to enhance their imagination.

Painting
Provide paint trays, large sheets of paper and fabric pieces, plus a range of 'tools', e.g. small pieces of wood, sponges, screwed-up newspaper 'rosettes', conventional paintbrushes and old toothbrushes. Encourage children to create artwork to enhance different learning environments, e.g. sails or shields for the role play area; a basket of treasure to support counting and recognition of shape in the mathematical area...

WHO SHALL I BE TODAY?

Role play
Ask children to help you set up the role play area to accommodate all the characters that they want to be, e.g. you could make a pirate ship with planks balanced on milk crates and painted fabric for sails, or perhaps you could tackle building a castle, collecting as many props as you and the children can find.

Creative design
Provide long strips of card for making hats, tiaras and crowns to support children's role play. Add shiny foil papers, jewels and confetti for them to decorate and enhance their creations.

For additional resources, visit collins.co.uk/CPMEYFS/download
© 2021 HarperCollinsPublishers Ltd

Who shall I be today?

MUSICAL LEARNING

Dressing up

Find two 'pirate' items from the role play area and use these to model the first verse of this song, inviting the children to join in with the repeated words and phrases, e.g. 'A pirate? A pirate?' Adapt the third line of the verse for the costume ideas/props you have available. Encourage children to select other dressing-up items and together create new verses about different characters, e.g. princess or astronaut (see additional verses below). Depending on your group, it may be more appropriate to start with the additional verses or children's ideas.

Being someone new

Model singing the song or all sing along with the recording, adding the claps that follow the lines: 'We like dressing up' and 'Who will you be?' (the recording makes these beats very clear and easy to follow). Once this clapping pattern is established, try stamping feet or invite children to choose a percussion instrument or other soundmaker to play instead of the claps.

Two friends dress up as pirates and find some unusual treasure. (See page 52.)
Let's find treasure refers to another story, *All aboard the pirate ship*, which is available in the online resources.

SONG

Dressing up

Melody: *There's a hole in my bucket*

It's a good day for dressing up,
For dressing up, for dressing up,
It's a good day for dressing up,
Now who will I be?

Shall I look like a pirate?
A pirate? A pirate?
With an eyepatch and parrot,
Yes, that's who I'll be!

It's a good day for dressing up,
For dressing up, for dressing up,
It's a good day for dressing up,
Now who will I be?

Additional verses:

Shall I look like a princess?
A princess? A princess?
With a cloak and tiara,
Yes, that's who I'll be!

It's a good day for dressing up,
For dressing up, for dressing up,
It's a good day for dressing up,
Now who will I be?

Shall I look like an astronaut?
An astronaut? An astronaut?
With a helmet and space boots,
Yes, that's who I'll be!

It's a good day for dressing up,
For dressing up, for dressing up,
It's a good day for dressing up,
Now who will I be?

SONG

Being someone new

We like dressing up [clap] some of the time
'Cause it's good being someone new!
We like dressing up [clap] some of the time
'Cause it's good being someone new!
Who will you be? [clap] Who will you be? [clap]
Dressing up is fun to do.
Who will you be? [clap] Who will you be? [clap]
Dressing up is fun for me and you!

For additional resources, visit collins.co.uk/CPMEYFS/download
© 2021 HarperCollinsPublishers Ltd

Who shall I be today?

ONLINE RESOURCES
Home learning

Stories
Let's find treasure
All aboard the pirate ship

Audio
Dressing up (song)
Being someone new (song)

Image
Pirate characters

AGES 3-4

COMMUNICATION AND LANGUAGE

Show children how to use a variety of mouth movements to make different sounds such as blowing, sucking, tongue-clicking or lip-smacking. Encourage children to experiment with vocal sounds in their play, to represent characters or animals. (This developmental activity can be linked to other starting points, where appropriate.)

PERSONAL, SOCIAL AND EMOTIONAL DEVELOPMENT

Create wooden spoon characters linked to your current dressing-up characters with happy, sad and cross faces. You could use both sides of the spoons for contrasting emotions, characters or colours. Encourage children to use these to express how they are feeling. These 'puppets' will help children who have communication and language difficulties.

PHYSICAL DEVELOPMENT

Devise a physical challenge for your children linked to their dressing-up characters, e.g. lay a plank of wood on a large piece of blue fabric, or balance it securely on two milk crates, to span a paddling pool full of water. Encourage children to 'walk the plank', landing safely on dry land or splashing into the shark-infested ocean, or to escape from a tower by means of a bridge that spans the moat!

LITERACY

After singing the song *Dressing up* ask the children to imagine they could be any character. Talk to them about who they would be and what they would wear!

MATHEMATICS

Collect six empty cardboard cylinders with lids. Print off pictures of your current dressing-up characters to stick on the front (for pirate characters, see online resources). Create a pyramid by placing three cylinders on the lowest stack, two on the next and one on the top. Ask children to throw a ball at the stack and count how many they knock down.

UNDERSTANDING THE WORLD

Before embarking on the activity, hide or bury treasure in your outside area and make a map with a set of 'pirate clues'. Read the story *Let's find treasure*, share the map and then invite children to find the treasure left by pirates.

EXPRESSIVE ARTS AND DESIGN

Support the children to make sparkly shakers by using funnels and teaspoons to part-fill small plastic bottles with a selection of jewels, small pieces of foil, tiny shells and eco-glitter. Secure the contents by replacing the lids and use the shakers to accompany the songs *Dressing up* and *Being someone new*.

Who shall I be today?

AGES 4-5

ONLINE RESOURCES
Home learning
Stories
Let's find treasure
All aboard the pirate ship
Audio
Dressing up (song)
Being someone new (song)
Image
Shadow theatre example

Notes

COMMUNICATION AND LANGUAGE

During role play, talk with children about their adopted characters (this activity could be linked to any characters). Discuss how they could change their voices by exaggerating their facial expressions and mouth shapes to change their vocal sounds, e.g. making them higher or lower, quieter or louder. Try recording the children during their play using an app or device that can distort voices in interesting ways and play recorded sounds backwards. Listen to the recordings and encourage children to talk about the changes they hear.

PERSONAL, SOCIAL AND EMOTIONAL DEVELOPMENT

Collect empty plastic bottles and encourage children to write a message to someone special. They place the message in the bottle to give to their special person.

PHYSICAL DEVELOPMENT

In the outdoor area, chalk six 'island' shapes about half a metre apart. Place 'treasure' on each island, e.g. silver fir cones and gold paint-sprayed pebbles, and explain to the children that these are the islands visited by pirates during their sea voyages. Encourage children to jump from island to island, collecting as much treasure as they can carry, without wetting their feet or falling into the sea!

LITERACY

Ask children to design a party invitation to a fancy-dress event. You could provide images of their favourite characters to cut out and stick onto the invitations with their own drawings and writing.

MATHEMATICS

Spray 20 pebbles with gold paint to make 'gold nuggets'. Number them 1 to 20 and place them in a treasure chest. Set simple challenges for children to follow, e.g. order numbers 1 to 10, place four pebbles in a square and guess how many there are before counting them, find some even numbers or divide the collection of 'gold nuggets' in half.

UNDERSTANDING THE WORLD

Use children's role play to expand their knowledge and understanding of the lives of people around them and their roles in society. Help children to recognise similarities and differences between their lives and the lives of people long ago, or those living in a different part of the world, or people of a different culture.

EXPRESSIVE ARTS AND DESIGN

Help children to create a shadow theatre using a large cardboard box, white tissue paper and a torch (see online resources). Encourage children to make their own shadow puppets and props fixed onto lollipop sticks or chopsticks to tell their own stories.

For additional resources, visit collins.co.uk/CPMEYFS/download
© 2021 HarperCollinsPublishers Ltd

LET'S GO GREEN!

You might like to introduce this starting point by using this image (see online resources) and a recycling bucket filled with plastic bottles, paper and cardboard.

Talk with children about the materials that we throw away and where these come from. Talk about the ways in which we can protect our world by recycling some materials, using them again and again.

Discuss which materials can be recycled and how everyone can help to do this, and what will happen if we don't look after our planet.

ENHANCING CONTINUOUS PROVISION

Play dough
Make play dough without any colour and add finely-chopped herbs such as rosemary or basil, which have strong scents. Introduce natural resources such as sticks, shells, stones and fir cones for children to add and press into their dough.

Water
Create a 'water wall' using perforated containers and other water-carrying items: collect colanders, funnels and water wheels and adapt plastic jugs, bottles and cups by making holes in each base; connect these to a wall or fence using lengths of tubing, hosepipe or guttering (see online resources). If this is impractical, the items could be fixed to a robust board, making the activity portable.

Sand
Make a pair of sand scales for children to use in their play: use a strong coat hanger and attach two plastic containers to each side of the cross bar with string (see online resources).

Small world and construction
Ask parents and carers to collect cardboard tubes, cylinders and large pieces of cardboard for children to bring in to use in construction play.

Painting
Fill small plastic bottles with coloured paint and encourage children to use these to squirt patterns onto pieces of paper. Offer cardboard tubes as well so that children can roll and spread the paint to achieve interesting images.

LET'S GO GREEN!

Role play
Involve your local community by asking people to collect empty plastic milk bottles or cartons for making milk bottle houses, and egg boxes to construct a house or castle. These can be used to enhance the role play area (see online resources).

Creative design
Gather items destined for the recycling bin. Work with children to create a huge robot that will become a symbol of your setting's commitment to reusing and recycling. You could use items mentioned in the song, Recycled robot.

For additional resources, visit collins.co.uk/CPMEYFS/download
© 2021 HarperCollinsPublishers Ltd

Let's go green!

MUSICAL LEARNING

Recycled robot
Sing the song. Once it is familiar, encourage children to move their heads and limbs making jerky, robotic actions. Invite a small group to provide an accompaniment played on recycled soundmakers (see online resources). Model playing your soundmaker on the pulse: some children may be able to copy this pattern.

Let's recycle!
Enjoy listening to the recording of this song with its rhythmic backing. When children are familiar with the song, encourage them to improvise their own accompaniment on recycled or junk instruments.

Concerto for robotic piano and strings
Encourage the children to imagine they are robots working in a recycling factory whilst listening to the music, e.g. they could explore the music by:
- Standing on the spot, moving legs and arms stiffly but rhythmically one at a time as if every limb is made of metal.
- Moving in straight lines, walking with the same stiff actions and moving their head from side to side. (Some children may manage to move to the strong beat or pulse.)
- Bending their bodies at the waist with heads hanging low when they hear the melody moving downwards, then standing again when the melody climbs upwards.
- In pairs, passing imaginary objects to and fro with jerky arms and heads.

SONG

Recycled robot   5

Melody: *The hokey cokey*

My head's a cardboard box,
A cardboard box,
Sticks for legs and
Paper bags for socks.
My eyes are made from bottle tops,
My tummy is a bin,
My mouth's an empty tin!
I'm your recycled robot,
I'm your recycled robot,
I'm your recycled robot,
I am your recycled friend!

SONG

Let's recycle!   6

Lots of rubbish that we throw away
Could be recycled for another day.
Plastic bottles, jars and tins
Need to go in the recycling bin!

Your old T-shirts and your worn-out shoes
Could be recycled into something new!
Gran's old jumpers, Grandpa's socks
Need to go in the recycling box!

Lots of rubbish that we throw away
Could be recycled for another day.
Plastic bottles, jars and tins
Need to go in the recycling bin!

LISTENING MUSIC

**Stephen Chadwick:
Concerto for robotic piano
and strings** 7

A futuristic repetitive robotic piece for piano, prepared piano and strings.

Let's go green!

ONLINE RESOURCES
Home learning

Audio
- Recycled robot (song)
- Let's recycle! (song)
- Concerto for robotic piano and strings (listening)

Images
- Plastic milk bottle windsock
- Classroom percussion instruments: scrapers

AGES 3-4

COMMUNICATION AND LANGUAGE

Collect hollow containers and packaging items, e.g. cardboard boxes, cylinders with lids, empty milk bottles and plastic vegetable trays. Encourage children to 'drum' these with wooden spoons or sticks, and observe how well children listen and respond to each other's explorations.

PERSONAL, SOCIAL AND EMOTIONAL DEVELOPMENT

Start a compost bin with the children, into which they add any vegetable or fruit waste from their daily snacks. You could contact your local authority to ask if they would sponsor your provision by donating a compost bin.

PHYSICAL DEVELOPMENT

Use empty plastic milk bottles and ribbons or crêpe paper strips to make windsocks (see online resources). Encourage children to run around holding up their windsocks and ask them to observe how the streamers react in the wind.

LITERACY

With the children, mix soil, water and a touch of washing-up liquid in a robust pot or large baking tray. Encourage children to 'mark-make' in the mud. Depending on each child's stage of development, these might be simple marks, letters or possibly even an image of the recycling logo!

MATHEMATICS

With the children, fill a basket with twigs and number ten cardboard tubes (or other cylinder containers) from 1 to 10. Encourage children to place the corresponding number of twigs into each tube. As children progress, encourage them to total the content of two tubes, counting the twigs to support the activity. When the total is higher than 10, help children to write the number on a new tube and count the twigs as they transfer them.

UNDERSTANDING THE WORLD

With children's help, fill a number of cardboard tubes or other small recyclable containers with peat-free compost. Provide a choice of seeds for children to sow in their biodegradable pots, e.g. lettuce, pak choi, beans or cress. Label them and stand them in a tray. Encourage children to nurture their seedlings, make regular checks and talk about their growth, then enjoy eating their home-grown produce!

EXPRESSIVE ARTS AND DESIGN

Encourage children to explore percussion instruments that make scraping sounds, e.g. cabasa, guiro or wooden agogo (see online resources). Then invite children to play plastic bottles that have a ridged surface with a variety of 'scrapers', e.g. lollipop sticks, chopsticks, twigs, wooden, metal and plastic spoons, etc. and to choose their preferred sound or 'timbre' to play to accompany the songs *Recycled robot* and *Let's recycle!*

Let's go green!

AGES 4-5

COMMUNICATION AND LANGUAGE

Place a few recyclable items on the floor. Ask each child in turn to describe one item and invite the others to guess which one is being described.

PERSONAL, SOCIAL AND EMOTIONAL DEVELOPMENT

Display the *Let's go green!* image and talk with children about single-use plastics and their impact on the level of waste in landfill sites. Bury a piece of plastic alongside a piece of paper and check after a few weeks to see what has happened. Encourage the children to think about what they could use instead of 'throwaway' plastic to be more environmentally friendly.

PHYSICAL DEVELOPMENT

In the outside area, make a jumbled pile of four kinds of recyclable materials: plastic, metal, cardboard and fabric. Position four containers a distance from the pile, and label each with the name and image of one of the materials. Use a stopwatch to time children sorting the items individually or as a team.

LITERACY

Sing the song *Recycled robot* and talk about the materials used to make the robot. Ask children if they have ever put these packaging items in their recycling bin. Can they write a list of alternative materials that could be used for the robot's eyes, mouth, socks and legs?

MATHEMATICS

Make a 3 x 3 grid using sticks (see online resources). Provide ample quantities of natural resources such as shells, pebbles or leaves and set appropriate mathematical challenges, e.g. fill each square with four objects; choose a number between 1 and 9 and place this total in every square; make a repeating pattern in each square. As children develop, encourage them to place the objects into five and then ten frames to help them recognise the 'tens structure' of the number system.

UNDERSTANDING THE WORLD

Talk to the children about recycling. Gather a large number of plastic and metal items, e.g. plastic bowls, trays and bottles; metal cutlery, biscuit tins and baking trays. Provide magnets and ask children to sort the items into metal and non-metal. (There will be interesting discussions if you include items made of aluminium or silver, which are not 'attracted' to magnets!)

EXPRESSIVE ARTS AND DESIGN

Encourage children to explore percussion instruments that make sounds by shaking or tapping, e.g. maracas, woodblocks or claves (see online resources), and listen to the sounds produced. Gather recyclable materials, e.g. cardboard or plastic boxes and bottles and help children make their own 'shakers' and 'tappers' (roll newspaper sheets to make 'sticks'). Invite children to use these to accompany the songs *Recycled robot* and *Let's recycle!*

ONLINE RESOURCES
Home learning

Audio
Recycled robot (song)
Let's recycle! (song)
Concerto for robotic piano and strings (listening)

Images
Let's go green! image
3 x 3 stick grid
Classroom percussion instruments: shakers and tappers

Notes

BUSY CITY

Display the image (see online resources). Children who live in a city will be used to its relentless, busy pace, but those living in more rural settings may not have experienced the sounds and sights of a city coming to life at night, with its noise, bustle, and dazzling lights.

Talk with children about what they like and don't like about where they live, discussing the different experiences of living in a city compared to living in a small rural community.

ENHANCING CONTINUOUS PROVISION

Play dough
Make some brightly-coloured 'flubber' (see online resources). Provide pots of eco-glitter for the children to add to the 'flubber' to add some city sparkle. Supply a number of wheeled vehicles to drive through the flubber and make tracks to enrich creative play and stimulate language.

Water
Make underwater magic sand (see online resources) and encourage children to use this to create a magical underwater city.

Sand
Add lots of vehicles and wooden blocks to the sand tray and invite children to build their own busy city, complete with roads for fast cars.

Small world and construction
Encourage the children to use blocks, construction and small-world toys to create their own city.

Painting
Fill each section of a bun tin with fluorescent or brightly coloured paint. Pinch cotton wool balls with clothes pegs and place one in each colour. Encourage children to produce bright, busy paintings.

BUSY CITY

Role play
Ask children to help you set up an outdoor street café. Create a menu together, gather cutlery and crockery and provide notebooks so that children can take down customers' orders.

Creative design
Provide bread, spread and fillings for children to make sandwiches for 'staff' to sell in the street café in their role play.

Busy city

MUSICAL LEARNING

Living in the city
Play the recording or sing the song and encourage the children to walk along an imaginary city street waving to each other as they pass by. Some may be able to walk to the strong beat, especially if you model the action. Learn to sing the song through repetition. Invite a small group to choose instruments or soundmakers to create a noisy, bustling city accompaniment.

Crazy city
Listen to the rap and encourage children to move to the irresistible beat, joining in when they can with the words. Invite children to choose instruments and soundmakers that suggest the noise and bustle of city life to play with the rap. Some children may be able to play in time with the pulse. Try modelling the rap without the backing and invite a group to play their own city accompaniment!

Galop
Encourage the children to explore the music imagining they are in a busy city, e.g.
- Walking briskly in straight lines, starting and stopping like vehicles and changing direction using their arms to indicate left and right.
- Riding invisible bikes, using high stepping knees to pedal, holding hands out on handlebars, steering and changing direction.
- Driving cars or buses, starting slowly and getting up to speed, beeping the horn and stopping at traffic lights.
- Being a pedestrian waiting at the lights then crossing the road, looking both ways.
- Directing the traffic by standing still and using both arms to stop and start the cars, turning their head to check left and right for cars on the side roads.

SONG

Living in the city 8

Melody: *This old man*

People walk
Down the street,
Stop and chat with
Friends they meet,
"Tell me how's your granny?
Say I said 'Hello!'"
City neighbours
On the go!

RAP

Crazy city  9

Crazy old city,
Busy old place.
Noises all around us,
People in your face!
Cars whizzing everywhere
Driving really fast,
Buses pulling in and out,
Bikes racing past!

Crazy old city,
Busy old place.
Noises all around us,
People in your face!
Children going off to school,
Grown-ups rushing round,
Trains rumble on their tracks
To another town!

LISTENING MUSIC

**Dmitry Kabalevsky:
Galop from The comedians**   10

A musical frenzy – a fast-paced orchestral piece with lots of percussion.

For additional resources, visit collins.co.uk/CPMEYFS/download
© 2021 HarperCollinsPublishers Ltd

 Busy city

ONLINE RESOURCES

Home learning

Audio
Living in the city (song)
Crazy city (rap)
Galop (listening)
City sounds
Country sounds

Image
City life photos

Notes

AGES 3-4

COMMUNICATION AND LANGUAGE

Listen to the recordings of life in a busy city contrasted with those of the countryside (*City sounds* and *Country sounds* – see online resources). Ask children to tell you what they hear and what these sounds tell them about the two dissimilar places.

PERSONAL, SOCIAL AND EMOTIONAL DEVELOPMENT

Help children to set out chairs to create the interior of a train carriage or aeroplane cabin. Support them in taking turns to board both forms of transport and making tickets or refreshments ready for the journey.

PHYSICAL DEVELOPMENT

Provide a number of large cardboard boxes to build a city. Encourage children to try to make the buildings taller than themselves and support them as they work out ways to construct their buildings to stand as high as possible.

LITERACY

Perform the *Crazy city* rap. Talk with children about the vehicles mentioned and find out which ones they have experienced. Support children in finding words and perhaps images of other forms of transport found in a busy city, e.g. prams, buggies, motorbikes, trams, rickshaw bikes, vans, lorries, underground trains/Metro.

MATHEMATICS

Ask children to help you make a car park, either on a large piece of card or with chalked spaces in the outside area. Number the parking bays 1 to 6 and allocate the same numbers to small cars or sit-and-ride vehicles and invite children to park vehicles in the corresponding bays.

UNDERSTANDING THE WORLD

Place a selection of photographs of famous city places in the block play area (see online resources). Select some of London, such as Big Ben and Buckingham Palace, or those found in your nearest city, including a tower block and high street shops. Use these to begin conversations about city landmarks and to inspire children's creative buildings (see Physical development).

EXPRESSIVE ARTS AND DESIGN

Place a very large sheet of paper in the outside area with a selection of large wheeled vehicles. Provide a selection of paints in shallow trays and invite children to wheel or drive their vehicles through the paint and onto the paper to make their own tracks and roads.

Busy city

AGES 4-5

COMMUNICATION AND LANGUAGE

Play the game, 'Say and spray', with the children. Fill small spray bottles with water and chalk some 'busy city' words in the outdoor area; once a child has correctly sounded out and said a word, they may erase it by spraying water on it. Encourage children to choose their own words to write, say and spray!

PERSONAL, SOCIAL AND EMOTIONAL DEVELOPMENT

Talk with children about where they live. Is it a city, town or village? Invite them to talk about the differences between these different locations. Ask children who don't live in a city if they have ever visited one. Encourage children to talk about what they like most about where they live and what they would like to change.

PHYSICAL DEVELOPMENT

Make or draw a road in the outside area and help children to make red, amber and green circle signs to use as traffic lights. Divide the children into groups: some to be traffic lights and others to run around the road as vehicles obeying the signs – they run when the sign is green, walk when it is amber and stop when it is red.

LITERACY

Create a set of city 'story stones' by sticking photos or drawings (see online resources) of 'city features' onto large pebbles, e.g. taxi, train, bus, blocks of flats, places of worship, etc. Use these to stimulate story creation and encourage children to share their ideas with you.

MATHEMATICS

Invite children to build skyscrapers using construction materials, and use these to stimulate mathematical discussion, e.g. talk about the different two- and three-dimensional shapes that children have used in their buildings and count the number of storeys, modelling positional language to expand their vocabulary as opportunities arise.

UNDERSTANDING THE WORLD

Talk with children about their nearest city and find out if they have ever visited it. Talk about some of the major UK and world cities and their best-known features. You could create a montage of photographs of these cities to share with the children.

EXPRESSIVE ARTS AND DESIGN

Provide black paper, fluorescent paint and straws, and invite children to blow the paint in all directions to represent city lights in the night sky.

ONLINE RESOURCES
Home learning
Audio
Living in the city (song)
Crazy city (rap)
Galop (listening)
Image
City features for story stones

Notes

For additional resources, visit collins.co.uk/CPMEYFS/download
© 2021 HarperCollinsPublishers Ltd

BEYOND THE STARS

Space is a really exciting concept for children. If at all possible, introduce it to coincide with a current space mission – you could then show the children a 'news item' either from a newspaper or TV.

Print off and display this image (see online resources), show it on a whiteboard, or project other images of the moon, stars and planets for children to see. Use the images to stimulate discussion. Talk with children about day and night and encourage parents to go out with their child in the evening to look at the moon and stars in the night sky. Talk about space and how astronauts travelled to the moon in a space rocket. Introduce some of the names of the planets, particularly Mars, and talk about the characteristics of the moon.

ENHANCING CONTINUOUS PROVISION

Play dough
Make black play dough and add eco-glitter. Provide star-, circle- and other space-shaped cutters for children to create their own 'universe'. A piece of dark, silky fabric could be supplied for children to display their universe.

Water
Add colour, eco-glitter and plastic star shapes to the water and introduce balls of varying sizes to represent 'moons' and 'planets'. Encourage the children to use 'space language' as they move the 'stars' and 'planets' around the water 'galaxy'.

Sand
Bury 'moon rocks' in the sand for children to find: these could be painted or gold-sprayed pebbles or items covered in foil.

Small world and construction
Encourage children to build a space station for their favourite small world toys to live in. They could also make spacesuits out of silver foil for the astronauts.

Painting
Place a photo of a space rocket (see online resources) in the painting area and ask children to look carefully at all the different parts. Encourage children to use these observations to inspire their own paintings.

BEYOND THE STARS

Role play
Provide a large cardboard box, a pair of red trainers, a red T-shirt, and a space hopper or box rocket for the role play area and invite children to recreate their own version of Zigi's journey to Mars. (See story page 52.)

Creative design
Collect cardboard boxes and rolls and provide glue, paint, tissue, silver foil and crêpe paper for children to make their own rockets. Provide a bigger box so that children have the opportunity to make a larger rocket for use in the role play area.

For additional resources, visit collins.co.uk/CPMEYFS/download
© 2021 HarperCollinsPublishers Ltd

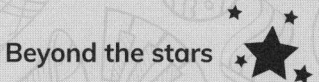

Beyond the stars

MUSICAL LEARNING

Space hopper take me to Mars

Ask children to imagine that they are sitting astride a space hopper. Sing the song and model bouncing on the strong beat or pulse. Encourage the children to copy. Once the song is familiar, invite children to join in with the two claps at the end of the first, second and final lines of each verse. Explore substituting other body percussion sounds for the claps.

Rocket ride

Sing the song, and encourage the children to let their voices slide upwards from low to high on the word 'Whoosh!'. Emphasise the rising pitch with a physical action, raising hands high. Demonstrate this upward pitch slide by running a beater along the bars of a glockenspiel or chime bar set from left to right (low to high). Invite children to explore percussion or soundmakers to find their own 'whooshing' sound to add to the song.

Music of the starry night

Encourage the children to explore the music by:
- Blowing bubbles with different sized blowing rings (or borrow a bubble machine), noticing how they float and travel in the air very lightly, then popping the bubbles when they hear loud crashes.
- Making light, floating movements in the air, focussing on different body parts: fingers, hands, arms, feet, legs and even whole bodies.
- Travelling and turning on tiptoe steps, moving in slow motion as if weighing nothing – just like the bubbles!

 STORY
Zigi bounces to Mars 11

A boy rides his space hopper and finds new friends on Mars. (See page 52.)

SONG

Space hopper take me to Mars   12

Melody: *Hickory dickory dock*

Space hopper take me to Mars. [clap clap]
Yes, bounce me and fly me to Mars. [clap clap]
I've heard it said
The planet's red.
Space hopper take me to Mars. [clap clap]

Space hopper take me back home. [clap clap]
Yes, bounce me and fly me back home. [clap clap]
Now Mars is fine
But it's breakfast time!
Space hopper take me back home. [clap clap]

SONG

Rocket ride   13

Whoosh! We're riding in a rocket.
Whoosh! We're zooming into space.
Whoosh! We're faster than a jet plane.
Look down! Look around and see the stars!

LISTENING MUSIC

George Crumb:
Music of the starry night (extract)
from **Music for a summer evening**
(Makrokosmos III)   14

A contemporary piece for piano and percussion with strange and eerie sound effects that are 'out of this world'!

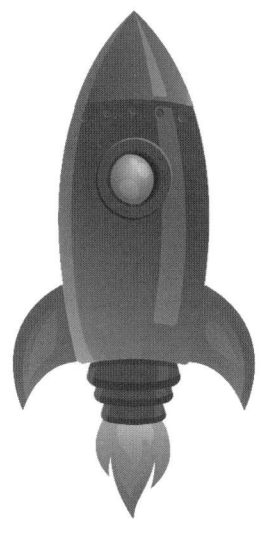

For additional resources, visit collins.co.uk/CPMEYFS/download
© 2021 HarperCollinsPublishers Ltd

17

Beyond the stars

ONLINE RESOURCES

Home learning

Story
Zigi bounces to Mars

Audio
Space hopper take me to Mars (song)
Rocket ride (song)
Music of the starry night (listening)

Image
Earth and space

Template
Paper aeroplane

AGES 3-4

COMMUNICATION AND LANGUAGE

Sing or play the song *Rocket ride* and ask what the children think it would be like to ride in a rocket. What sort of stars and planets might they pass on the way to Mars? Help children to think up some imaginary names for planets, modelling the activity initially by using children's names, e.g. Ajay-star; Katie-moon; Annie-Tannie.

PERSONAL, SOCIAL AND EMOTIONAL DEVELOPMENT

Share the story *Zigi bounces to Mars* and discuss how Zigi felt when he reached Mars and met some new green friends. Ask children if they have ever been hungry like Zigi.

PHYSICAL DEVELOPMENT

Chalk moon and star shapes in the outside area and place a soundmaker in each one. You could include robust percussion for this activity: instruments such as woodblocks, claves or bells, but not the more fragile 'skin' instruments such as tambourines. Ask children to 'fly' around the stars and moons in their rockets and when you call out "Moon landing!" they land in a shape and make 'space music'. When you say, "Rockets fly!" they set off again to move around the 'galaxy'.

LITERACY

Share the story *Zigi bounces to Mars* and talk about his journey. Encourage children to think about how Zigi would have reacted if there were no Martian creatures to play with – would he still have enjoyed his space visit?

MATHEMATICS

Help children to make A4 paper aeroplanes (see online resources) to represent space rockets. Encourage children to count down from ten before launching their rockets into space.

UNDERSTANDING THE WORLD

Collect and mix up various items, such as cars and trees from small world toys with furniture from your dolls' house, etc. Add stars and rockets and ask children to sort the items between two pictures, one of Earth and one of space (see online resources).

EXPRESSIVE ARTS AND DESIGN

Place large pieces of black paper on the ground of the outside area or attach them to a fence. Provide pots of slightly watered-down paints and thick paint brushes and invite children to make a 'splatter paint' galaxy!

For additional resources, visit collins.co.uk/CPMEYFS/download
© 2021 HarperCollinsPublishers Ltd

Beyond the stars

ONLINE RESOURCES
Home learning
Story
Zigi bounces to Mars
Audio
Space hopper take me to Mars (song)
Rocket ride (song)
Music of the starry night (listening)
Space sounds
Templates
Rocket list
Paper aeroplane
Moon sand recipe

Notes

AGES 4-5

COMMUNICATION AND LANGUAGE

Sit in a circle and ask one child to start a 'moon whisper': this could be a word, an idea from the story, or perhaps something invented. Pass the whisper around the circle and when it arrives at the last child, ask them to say the 'moon whisper' out loud, allowing everyone to compare it to the original.

PERSONAL, SOCIAL AND EMOTIONAL DEVELOPMENT

Listen to the compilation of space sounds (see online resources) and listen to children's responses. Do they find the music scary? Or exciting? Does it make them think of rockets or aliens? Does it make them want to dance? Encourage children to respond in any way that they wish.

PHYSICAL DEVELOPMENT

Play a version of 'Simon says' with a group of children, but change the name to 'Saturn says', e.g. "Saturn says take ten steps to Mars" or "Saturn says jump as high as you can to reach the moon." Children may only respond if you begin with "Saturn says…"

LITERACY 11

After listening to the story *Zigi bounces to Mars*, ask children to write a list of items that they would take on a journey to that planet in a rocket (see online resources).

MATHEMATICS

Make paper aeroplanes to represent rockets (see online resources) and invite small groups of children to throw their rocket planes as far as they can from a given starting point. Ask each child to measure the distance travelled by counting in giant footsteps and to record the result. Children can then work out whose rocket has travelled the greatest distance.

UNDERSTANDING THE WORLD

Ask children to help you make 'moon sand' by mixing sand, cornflour, paint powder, eco-glitter and water in a deep plastic box or 'Tuff tray' (see online resources). When the mixture is completely integrated, make the surface really smooth. Collect different-sized pebbles and small rocks and ask children to drop these onto the mixture to replicate the craters found on the moon's surface.

EXPRESSIVE ARTS AND DESIGN

Ask children to create their own space creatures using clay. This activity should be unsupported, relying solely on each child's imagination.

For additional resources, visit collins.co.uk/CPMEYFS/download
© 2021 HarperCollinsPublishers Ltd

WHEN SNOWFLAKES FALL

Most children love snow: building snowmen, making snow angels or running across a snowy field to leave their footprints behind. It is one of the times when Early Years Practitioners need to be totally spontaneous, forget planned activities and take full advantage of any snowfall, enjoying it before it melts!

Obviously, the ideal time to introduce this starting point is when snow has fallen or is forecast, however, if snow doesn't appear (or you live somewhere that is unlikely to get snow), you could always bring in a bucket of fake snow or ice instead.

ENHANCING CONTINUOUS PROVISION

Play dough
Make some silky 'snow dough' (see online resources). Provide children with plastic snowflakes and pieces of patterned lace or fabric to add to the dough and provide eco-glitter and cutters, too.

Sand
Mix sand, silver eco-glitter and plastic snowflakes with shaving foam for the children to investigate. Add other objects that fit with this wintry theme to create interest and discussion, e.g. you could print, cut out and laminate images from the film *Frozen*.

Water
Freeze small 'wintry' or white objects such as snowflake confetti, eco-glitter or pieces of white lace in ice cubes and add these to the water tray. You could also add white ping-pong balls or pieces of sponge, or a large 'iceberg' made by filling a plastic box, such as an ice cream container, with water and freezing it.

Painting
Freeze water in small flat trays and encourage children to paint on the icy surfaces. Provide sheets of paper so that children can make prints of their paintings.

Small world and construction
Encourage children to create a wintry scene in a 'Tuff' tray. Provide small world icebergs or clear glass 'pebbles' and add penguins, polar bears, snow ploughs or other objects that lend themselves to the theme. Make fake snow (see online resources), or use shredded paper, soap flakes, sugar or oats.

Role play
Supply winter clothes, boots and lengths of fine white material for winter-related role play. If you have a home corner, you could ask the children to help you make a cosy area with a fireplace, rug, cushions and blankets.

Creative design
Encourage children to make papier mâché and use it to make snow sculptures: soak toilet tissue in warm water then, once the paper is soft, show children how to squeeze out the water and add PVA glue.

WHEN SNOWFLAKES FALL

For additional resources, visit collins.co.uk/CPMEYFS/download
© 2021 HarperCollinsPublishers Ltd

When snowflakes fall

MUSICAL LEARNING

Snowflakes fall

The melody for this song has a very small range of just four notes, arranged largely in 'stepping' or next-door note patterns, which are useful for developing children's 'pitch-matching'. Model singing each line, inviting the children to copy. Once the song is familiar, invite children to think of other places where the snowflakes might land, e.g. on my chin, my coat, my mitts... and enjoy singing these new versions. You could also add fluttering snowflake fingers as you sing, or play gentle sounds on home-made shakers containing sparkly eco-glitter, plastic snowflakes or confetti.

Jack Frost's fingers

Model singing this song in a very 'spiky' voice, making each word detached and separate (the recording demonstrates this very clearly). Invite the children to join in and encourage a group to improvise on triangles, bells or even teaspoons tapped together to add atmospheric metallic sound effects to the song. Encourage children to be Jack Frost, pointing index fingers to paint imaginary icy designs in the air.

La campanella

Encourage the children to explore the music by:
- Standing still with arms and hands outstretched to catch the falling snowflakes.
- Walking about on tiptoes, moving their arms quickly and lightly with dancing 'snowflake' fingers.
- Twirling round on the spot like a snowflake and gradually sinking to settle on the ground.

 **POEM**
My snowman 15

On a snowy day, a boy builds a snowman in the garden. (See page 53.)

SONG
Snowflakes fall 16

Melody: *Pease pudding hot*

Snow's falling down,
Down from the sky.
Lands on my hat and I
Wonder why!

LISTENING MUSIC

Franz Liszt:
La campanella from **Grandes études de Paganini** (extract) 18

A twinkling piano piece with feather-light notes that dance and twirl over the keyboard.

SONG
Jack Frost's fingers 17

Jack Frost's painting all the window panes,
Makes them shine in wintertime!
Fingers painting ev'ry chilly night
Icy patterns all in white.

Jack Frost's painting ev'ry blade of grass,
Makes them shine in wintertime!
Fingers painting ev'ry chilly night
Icy patterns all in white.

Jack Frost's painting ev'ry garden wall,
Makes them shine in wintertime!
Fingers painting ev'ry chilly night
Icy patterns all in white.

Jack Frost's painting ev'ry little twig,
Makes them shine in wintertime!
Fingers painting ev'ry chilly night
Icy patterns all in white.

For additional resources, visit collins.co.uk/CPMEYFS/download
© 2021 HarperCollinsPublishers Ltd

When snowflakes fall

ONLINE RESOURCES

Home learning

Poem
My snowman

Audio
Snowflakes fall (song)
Jack Frost's fingers (song)
La campanella (listening)

Notes

AGES 3-4

COMMUNICATION AND LANGUAGE   15

Share the poem *My snowman*. Ask whether the children have played in the snow, built a snowman or made a snow angel. Talk about their experiences. Do they think all snowmen change when the weather warms up, like the one in the poem?

PERSONAL, SOCIAL AND EMOTIONAL DEVELOPMENT   16

Sing the song *Snowflakes fall* and talk with children about playing outside in cold and snowy weather. Can they think of other places where snowflakes might land? Try fitting these ideas into new verses. Do they prefer being outside when it's cold or when it's hot? Discuss the different clothes they would wear to keep warm in cold weather. How do children feel when they're extremely cold? What happens when their hands become cold? Do their fingers change colour?

PHYSICAL DEVELOPMENT

If you are fortunate enough to have a snowy day, make lots of footprints and snow tracks with the children. If there's no snow, ask children to make footprints by stepping into a tray of sand.

LITERACY

Fill trays with eco-glitter and flour and invite children to 'mark-make' in the snowy mixture. As they develop greater writing skills, encourage children to write the letters of their name or try some familiar words.

MATHEMATICS

Use small buckets or cut the tops off ten large plastic milk bottles and stick a snowman's head of screwed-up white paper onto each one. Number the snowmen from 1 to 10 and fill a basket with cotton wool balls. Invite children to place the correct number of 'snowballs' around each figure.

UNDERSTANDING THE WORLD

During the colder winter months, place different-sized containers of water in the outside area. Ask children to check them each day to see whether the water has frozen. Freeze flowers and leaves in cake tins with a little water, adding a string loop to each one. Hang the frozen discs around the outdoor area, asking children to watch to see if the discs melt, letting the flowers fall, or whether they remain frozen throughout the day.

EXPRESSIVE ARTS AND DESIGN

Add shaving foam to white paint and invite children to paint a picture of a melting snowman. Provide screwed-up pieces of black tissue paper for the snowman's eyes, with pieces of carrot, buttons and beads to add to their pictures.

For additional resources, visit collins.co.uk/CPMEYFS/download
© 2021 HarperCollinsPublishers Ltd

When snowflakes fall

AGES 4-5

COMMUNICATION AND LANGUAGE

Encourage children to make 'snow scenes' by putting eco-glitter, snowflakes and different small wintry objects into plastic bottles, then filling these with water and screwing the lids on tightly. Encourage children to shake their bottles and describe what they see.

PERSONAL, SOCIAL AND EMOTIONAL DEVELOPMENT

Cut out small circles in four different colours and attach a snowflake to each. You will need enough for one per child. Make up four questions (one for each colour), e.g. How would you feel if you woke up in the morning and saw snow outside your window? How would you build a snowman? Write a question on the back of each snowflake and distribute them to the children. Ask all children with matching coloured circles to get together and discuss their question.

PHYSICAL DEVELOPMENT

Cover a large dice or small square cardboard box with white paper and write actions on each side, e.g. 'spin like a snowflake' or 'curl up like a snowball' (see online resources). Invite one child to throw the cube and ask children to respond to the instruction lying uppermost.

LITERACY

Display the frost images (see online resources). Ask if children have ever played outside on frosty days and seen their breath look like clouds. Sing the song *Jack Frost's fingers* and explain who Jack Frost is. Ask children to choose a word from the song or think of their own wintry word and write the different letters on strips of paper. Join these strips up as links with a blank link between each letter, to make winter word chains (see online resources).

MATHEMATICS

Cut out a large circle of blue card. Divide each side into ten sections numbering one side 1 to 10 and the other 11 to 20 (see online resources). In each section children can draw, print or stick the corresponding number of snowflakes. Place snowflakes together in groups of 4 or 5 and ask children to subitise before counting.

UNDERSTANDING THE WORLD

Talk with children about water in its different forms (solid, liquid, gas) and the weather conditions that bring us snow and ice. Provide containers of warm, cold and icy water for children to investigate. You could show the photo or video of a geyser (see online resources), to show steam.

EXPRESSIVE ARTS AND DESIGN

Provide children with black and white paper, white and pale blue paint, silver and blue eco-glitter and forks to use as art tools. Encourage children to use these materials to create snowflake designs.

ONLINE RESOURCES
Home learning
Poem
My snowman
Audio
Snowflakes fall (song)
Jack Frost's fingers (song)
La campanella (listening)
Video
Geyser video
Images
Frost images
Winter word chains
Geyser image
Templates
Snowflake dice
Snowflake number card

Notes

For additional resources, visit collins.co.uk/CPMEYFS/download
© 2021 HarperCollinsPublishers Ltd

FABULOUS FOOD

The busy lifestyle followed by many families today often makes eating together more of a challenge, but sharing food with others has physical and social benefits. In this starting point we aim to help children understand where food comes from by introducing growing, choosing and buying nutritious food to be prepared and shared together.

Likes and dislikes are often established at a very early age so it is important to acquaint children with the wide range of ingredients that are available nowadays, to encourage exploration and to celebrate food from different cultures and climates.

ENHANCING CONTINUOUS PROVISION

Play dough
Invite children to make food that they would like to eat in a café out of salt-dough (see online resources). They might choose to make sandwiches, cakes or prawn crackers. Once the food is ready, bake the dough items until they are dried out. The children can then paint and varnish the food to use in their role play café (see Role play).

Water
Add chopped vegetables, e.g. carrots, peppers and peas to the water tray, along with uncooked rice and pasta. Provide several sets of plastic or wooden chopsticks, plenty of containers such as plastic tubs and bowls for children to use in their play, plus small woks or saucepans, sieves, spoons and ladles.

Sand
Add food colouring and just enough water to make the sand stick together. Place a selection of cake tins, patty tins, cupcake cases, mixing bowls and spoons to encourage children to make cakes and dishes of their choice.

Small world and construction
Add tractors, farm vehicles and a tray of soil to the small world area. Provide small baskets containing Brussels sprouts, carrot tops, radishes, broccoli, flowers, tiny potatoes and small plant pots for children to use in their play.

Painting
Provide flat trays containing different coloured paints, sheets of paper, a selection of fruit and vegetables and child-friendly knives. Model cutting the food safely, and encourage children to dip the pieces of fruit and vegetables into the paint to create their own works of art.

Role play
Turn the role play area into a café by providing resources such as plastic table cloths, crockery, cutlery, trays and menus plus note pads and pencils for taking orders. Talk with children about the types of food that they would like to see on the menu and make salt-dough food items (see Play dough) to paint and varnish to serve in the café.

Creative design
Having cooked Chinese-style egg noodles, rice, peas, sweetcorn and fried eggs beforehand, place each food in separate bowls in the creative area. Ask children to assemble items in an individual bowl to eat there and then, or to have for their lunch, and offer chopsticks for children to try out, too. (Follow the usual health and hygiene procedures for cooking with children set out in your setting's policy.)

FABULOUS FOOD

For additional resources, visit collins.co.uk/CPMEYFS/download
© 2021 HarperCollinsPublishers Ltd

Fabulous food

MUSICAL LEARNING

Yummy, yummy yum cha
Before listening to the song, talk about 'dim sum' and explain how these little dumplings are made – if possible, bring some in for everyone to try. Tell children what the song words mean and encourage them to join in singing the words 'dim sum', which are repeated frequently throughout the song. When children listen again, provide chopsticks and paper plates so that they can tap improvised accompaniments whilst they become more familiar with the melody and lyrics.

Noodle song
Before embarking on this musical activity, tell children what the words mean and, if possible, organise a fried noodle 'tasting', or, better still, share some vegetable chow mein (see online resources). Enjoy listening to the song, especially the sound of the Chinese instruments that play in the introduction and between repetitions of the song. Notice that the words 'chow mein' are repeated after every line, so encourage children to join in with this little phrase. The accessible melody and the remaining lyrics will be easily learnt as the song becomes familiar. Why not make simple noodle shakers to accompany the song (see online resources)?

STORY
Ai Lin cooks chow mein  19

Ai Lin helps her granny cook a delicious Chinese meal for their family. (See page 53.)

SONG
Yummy, yummy yum cha 20

Dim sum, dim sum gnaw joong yi,
Yat joong saam geen wai yum cha.
Dim sum, dim sum gnaw joong yi,
Cha siu baaw, haa gaaw, siu maai.

Yummy, yummy yum cha,
Yummy, yummy yum cha.

Dim sum, dim sum gnaw joong yi,
Yat joong saam geen wai yum cha.
Dim sum, dim sum gnaw joong yi,
Cha siu baaw, haa gaaw, siu maai.

Cha siu baaw, haa gaaw, siu maai.

Translation
Dim sum delights me,
One cup and three pieces makes a meal.
Dim sum delights me,
Roasted pork buns, prawn dumplings,
    meat dumplings.
What a yummy meal!

SONG
Noodle song 21

Wo ai chi chao mian,
Ni ai chi chao mian,
Ta ai chi chao mian,
Wai po de chao mian.

Wo ai chi chao mian,
Ni ai chi chao mian,
Shei bu ai chao mian?
Wai po de chao mian.

[Repeat]

Translation
I love to eat fried noodles,
You love to eat fried noodles,
They love to eat fried noodles,
Granny's fried noodles.

I love to eat fried noodles,
You love to eat fried noodles,
Who doesn't love to eat fried noodles?
Granny's fried noodles.

 **Fabulous food**

ONLINE RESOURCES
Home learning

Story
Ai Lin cooks chow mein

Audio
Yummy, yummy yum cha (song)
Noodle song (song)

Templates
Vegetable chow mein recipe
Fruit and vegetable graph

AGES 3-4

COMMUNICATION AND LANGUAGE

Place eight food items on a tray, e.g. ocra, potato, packet of pasta, etc. Show children the tray, encouraging them to look carefully and remember what they see. Ask them to look away while you cover one item with an opaque bowl. Encourage children to discuss together what is hidden.

PERSONAL, SOCIAL AND EMOTIONAL DEVELOPMENT

Prepare snack time food together in small groups. Encourage children to talk about foods they like and listen to each other's favourites. You could invite children to add savoury or sweet toppings to a cooked pizza base, or cut up fruit to make a fruit salad to share.

PHYSICAL DEVELOPMENT

Draw a chalk outline of a large tree or bush in the outside area. Ask children to help paint pebbles to represent fruit and arrange these on the outline. Place a basket a few metres away and ask children to collect the 'fruit', one piece at a time, and put them in the basket. Use a sand timer to see if children can complete the task before the sand all runs through.

LITERACY

Share the story *Ai Lin cooks chow mein* and talk about the two main characters. Has anyone helped their granny to cook food? What did they make? Has anyone ever tried Chinese food? What do they like best? You could make chow mein together, talking about the ingredients and flavours, and inviting children to try it and see whether they like it (see online resources).

MATHEMATICS

Provide a selection of pieces of different fruits and vegetables for the children to sample. For each one, cut out squares of appropriately-coloured paper to make a graph (see online resources). Invite children to sample all the fruit and vegetables and choose their favourite, then stick the corresponding coloured square onto the graph. When everyone has added their square, count up the totals, and agree which was the most popular item.

UNDERSTANDING THE WORLD

Talk with children about foods that people grow from seed in their allotments, gardens and greenhouses and share any experiences. Explain that some seeds can be sown directly in the ground, while others are germinated in trays and transplanted as seedlings. Try growing seed potatoes, cherry tomatoes or strawberries in your outdoor area in pots, hanging baskets or even carrier bags. Encourage children to nurture their plants.

EXPRESSIVE ARTS AND DESIGN

Provide a collection of different fruits and vegetables with chopping boards, child-friendly knives and cocktail sticks. Ask children to create a fruit and/or vegetable sculpture, e.g. a fruit rocket, a grape and tomato caterpillar or a melon boat... all of which they can enjoy eating later.

Fabulous food

AGES 4-5

ONLINE RESOURCES
Home learning

Story
Ai Lin cooks chow mein

Audio
Yummy, yummy yum cha (song)
Noodle song (song)

Notes

COMMUNICATION AND LANGUAGE

Place several food items in a string bag. Pass the bag round asking each child in turn to take out an item, say its name and try to think of a word beginning with the same sound. Challenge more able children to think of a word or nonsense word to rhyme with the name of the food item.

PERSONAL, SOCIAL AND EMOTIONAL DEVELOPMENT

Help children to use child-friendly knives to cut pieces of melon, strawberries, grapes, kiwi or any seasonal fruit and thread these on cocktail sticks or small bamboo skewers to make 'fruit kebabs' to share at snack time. Explain that some children may have different dietary requirements and ensure that the fruit kebabs accommodate the individual food needs of all their peers.

PHYSICAL DEVELOPMENT

Play the 'Bean game' in the outside area. Start by asking children to hop or stand on one leg. When you call out, "Runner beans", they run on the spot; "Jumping beans" means jump; "French beans", everyone replies, "Oh là là!"; "Broad beans", they stretch out their arms wide; "Beans on toast", they lie flat on the floor with arms and legs spread out; "Jelly beans", everyone wobbles about!

LITERACY

Put a selection of tins and packets of food into a shopping basket. Encourage children to look at the food items and try to work out what is inside, using the words and images on the tin or packet. More able readers may like to read the list of ingredients. Ask children to write a list of the five foods in the basket that they would most like to eat.

MATHEMATICS

Create a sweet shop by providing a number of bowls or jars, each containing different coloured sweets, with small paper bags and tweezers. Write out some 'customer' orders with specific requests and invite children to estimate the number of sweets in a bowl before counting out the correct number and colours of sweets to match each order. Ask children to write the customer's name on the front of the bag.

UNDERSTANDING THE WORLD

Talk with children about how food can be changed from one state to another by cooking or by processing it in some way, e.g. turning cream into butter. Invite children to make their own butter (individually or as a group): pour a large carton of whipping or double cream plus a pinch of salt into a plastic container with a lid and shake until butter is formed. Try and discuss the results!

EXPRESSIVE ARTS AND DESIGN

Remind children of the story *Ai Lin cooks chow mein* and bring in some of the ingredients, e.g. ginger root, garlic and pak choi. Provide a range of drawing materials and invite children to make observational drawings of the different ingredients after looking at them very carefully.

For additional resources, visit collins.co.uk/CPMEYFS/download
© 2021 HarperCollinsPublishers Ltd

A TALE FROM LONG AGO

Traditional tales are stories that have been told and retold over many years and passed down through the generations to become embedded in our culture. These well-known stories often have a magical element, sometimes exploring issues of right from wrong and usually following a clear structure. They are vitally important in supporting the development of young children's literacy skills.

There are many traditional tales to explore – we have chosen to focus on *The elves and the shoemaker*. You could introduce the starting point by wrapping up a copy of the book in brown paper with a big bow and leaving it for the children to find. It may be best to share the story of *The helpful elves* with the children (see page 54) before accessing the supporting activities. The songs and chant opposite also tell the story in its proper sequence.

ENHANCING CONTINUOUS PROVISION

Play dough
Have balls of play dough, small hammers and plenty of golf tees, so that children can replicate the elves hammering nails onto the shoes. Provide different lengths and colours of shoelaces for children to press into their dough.

Water
Fill the water container with soapy water and add a number of old shoes in different sizes and styles for children to use as containers and see how much water each shoe holds. (Try to get some with lace holes and some small wellies.)

Sand
Ask children to make a trail of footprints (barefoot or wearing shoes), either by walking through the sandpit or through a 'sand trail box', made by lining a long cardboard box with silver foil and filling with a small amount of sand (see online resources).

Small world and construction
Encourage children to make an 'elf' house or habitat, built either from construction materials or natural objects, such as logs, sticks, twigs, moss, stones or fir cones. Provide strips of fabric, too, to support the creation of these imaginary 'dwellings'.

Painting
Encourage children, wearing their outdoor shoes, to step into a tray of paint and then walk along strips of paper, leaving a trail of patterned footprints. Have a towel 'doormat' at the end for wiping shoes.

A TALE FROM LONG AGO

Role play
Create a shoe shop with your children's help. Collect shoe boxes, old shoes and shoe horns, then beg, borrow or make a foot slide to measure the length and width of children's feet (see online resources). Position a mirror facing a long, low stool for 'customers' to use when trying on shoes. You could link this activity to the story, *Cinderella* – when her stepsisters try to force their large feet into her dainty glass slipper!

Creative design
Introduce a planning element to your creative design area, linked to the story of *The helpful elves*. Encourage children to identify and talk about the different parts of a shoe: soles, straps, laces, buckles, Velcro, etc. Provide a design template (see online resources) for children to use to draw their design for some shoes for the elves to make.

For additional resources, visit collins.co.uk/CPMEYFS/download
© 2021 HarperCollinsPublishers Ltd

A tale from long ago

MUSICAL LEARNING

The shoemaker's piggy bank
Invite children to join in singing the song. The 'cuckoo' notes in the opening phrase, 'Is there any money', provide excellent opportunities for 'pitch-matching'. Accompany the final line: 'Shake, shake, what have we got?' either by shaking a piggy bank or playing maracas (shakers).

One pair of shoes
Model the chant until it is familiar, inviting children to join in with the repeated lines: 'One (two, three) pair(s) of shoes.' Invite a small group to play along to the strong beat in the backing track using claves or sticks.

Midnight
This song has echoing phrases, so model each line and encourage children to copy you for the echo. Invite a small group to choose suitable soundmakers or instruments to play with the repeating 'tick tock' lines.

Presents for the elves
The first line of the song has two phrases with repeated notes which provides another opportunity for some useful 'pitch-matching'. Once the song is established, try singing this song in two groups – one singing the shoemaker's verses; the other his wife's.

Impressions: III. To the point
Encourage children to imagine they are the elves from the story and explore the music by:
- Scampering around, leaping and jumping in all directions as the music darts about.
- Waving friendly greetings to each other as they meet.
- Sometimes standing still to pretend to hammer the soles onto the shoes, using a fist to beat on the other palm.

STORY
The helpful elves
Two little elves appear one night in the shoemaker's workshop…
(See page 54.)

SONG
The shoemaker's piggy bank

Is there any money in the piggy bank?
The piggy bank, the piggy bank?
Is there any money in the piggy bank?
Shake, shake, what have we got?

CHANT
One pair of shoes

He cut out the leather
And left it on the side.
He went up to bed,
He was very, very tired! (Yawn!)
Up next morning
And what did he find?
[ALL] *One pair of shoes, (Ooh!)
[ALL] *One pair of shoes, (Ah!)
[ALL] *One pair of shoes,
And they looked just fine!
"I'll put them in the window
And write out the price,

Everyone will want them
'Cause they look so nice!"

* Two pairs of shoes, etc.

SONG
Midnight

Melody: *Ring a ring 'o roses*

Leader: At the stroke of midnight,
Echo: At the stroke of midnight,
Leader: Tick tock,
Echo: Tick tock,
All: The elves arrived.

Found the bits of leather, (echo)
Tick tock, (echo)
They stitched the thread.

Found the nails and hammered, (echo)
Tick tock, (echo)
To fix the soles.

Then the shoes were finished, (echo)
Tick tock, (echo)
They left the shop.

SONG
Presents for the elves

Melody: *The farmer's in his den*

Shoemaker's wife:
Now, I will make some clothes,
The elves are wearing rags.
I'll make clothes for them,
Now, where's my sewing bag?

Now, green* is what I'll choose,
I think that colour's right.
I'll choose green for them,
They'll have new clothes tonight.

Shoemaker:
Now, I will make some shoes,
Their little feet look bare.
I'll make shoes for them,
I'll make them each a pair.

Now, red* is what I'll choose,
I think that colour's right.
I'll choose red for them,
They'll have new shoes tonight.

* Children to choose their own colours.

LISTENING MUSIC

Jennifer Higdon:
Impressions: III.
To the point (extract)

A contemporary piece for strings with exciting darting rhythms.

For additional resources, visit collins.co.uk/CPMEYFS/download
© 2021 HarperCollinsPublishers Ltd

A tale from long ago

ONLINE RESOURCES
Home learning

Story
The helpful elves

Audio
The shoemaker's piggy bank (song)
One pair of shoes (chant)
Midnight (song)
Presents for the elves (song)
Impressions: III. To the point (listening)

AGES 3-4

COMMUNICATION AND LANGUAGE   25

Make a collection of different footwear (shoes, boots and sandals in as many contrasting materials, sizes and styles as possible) and provide wooden spoons or sticks. Ask children to tap each shoe, listening to the different sounds produced. Talk with children about their 'shoe drumming' experiences. Ask questions such as: which made the loudest/quietest sound? Which sound did you like best? Can you find a few shoes to make a drumkit and play a pattern while we sing the song, *Midnight*?

PERSONAL, SOCIAL AND EMOTIONAL DEVELOPMENT   22

Remind children of the story of *The helpful elves* then talk with the children about how the elves helped the shoemaker and his wife. Ask children if they can think of any 'kind' action that they could do to help one of their friends or a member of their family.

PHYSICAL DEVELOPMENT   22

Provide an old colander and pipe cleaners for children to thread through the holes, replicating the elves' sewing actions as they stitched the new shoes in the story, *The helpful elves*.

LITERACY   22

Read the story *The helpful elves* and talk with children about the shoemaker and his wife – about their worry at having no money and how their lives were changed by the elves' kindness. Encourage children to 'mark-make' their thank you messages to the elves on old shoes or boots using chalk.

MATHEMATICS

Use your footwear collection (see Communication and Language) and invite children to find the longest and shortest shoe. Set other mathematical challenges, e.g. ask children to sort the shoes in different ways: by size order, colour, or by the type of fastening (i.e. buckle and strap, Velcro or laces, not forgetting those with no fastenings, e.g. flip-flops).

UNDERSTANDING THE WORLD

Collect outgrown or discarded boots and wellingtons. Parents/carers might supply these, or, alternatively, find these footwear items in charity shops. Fill these with peat-free compost and help children to sow herb and flower seeds, encouraging them to nurture their seedlings. Position the 'boot pots' in the outside area to add interest and colour.

EXPRESSIVE ARTS AND DESIGN

Cook spaghetti and place this in a tray to represent shoelaces. Provide spoons for children to stir various colourful paints and eco-glitter into the pasta. Talk with children about what happens when these are integrated. Children may prefer to use their hands to mix everything and some may also enjoy placing the colourful pasta strands onto paper to create their own pictures.

A tale from long ago

AGES 4-5

COMMUNICATION AND LANGUAGE

Share the story *The helpful elves* and ask the children who might have bought the new shoes that the elves made. Pose more questions, e.g. what sort of shoes might they have been? What colour was the leather? Who would have worn them? Were they worn for a special occasion?

PERSONAL, SOCIAL AND EMOTIONAL DEVELOPMENT

Ask children why they think the shoemaker and his wife stayed hidden in the story, *The helpful elves*. Why didn't they come out from behind the curtain and thank the elves face to face?

PHYSICAL DEVELOPMENT

Mark out a race track with different lanes, and position five shoes or boots spaced evenly along each lane. Each lane should also have a cardboard box positioned at the start. Divide the group of children into teams: the first child in each team runs to the first shoe and brings it back to the box, then to the second, then the third, etc. until all five shoes are gathered in the box. Invite those children waiting for their turn, to time their friends to see who finishes each heat in the fastest time and work out who is the overall winner.

LITERACY

Ask children to design a poster advertising a shoe sale; it could be of the shoes made by the elves in the story, *The helpful elves*. Talk with children about what information they would need to include, e.g. facts such as the date, the venue and the time of the sale.

MATHEMATICS

Challenge children to attach as many clothes pegs as possible to a trainer or boot. Ask children to record the number of pegs used and reveal the winner.

UNDERSTANDING THE WORLD

Show children images of different people and different types of footwear (see online resources) and ask the children to match the wearer to the footwear, e.g. dancer – ballet shoes; builder – heavy boots… Ask about their 'matches' and find out why they made these choices. Talk with children about the function of each shoe type and which materials have been used to make them.

EXPRESSIVE ARTS AND DESIGN

Provide a collection of different styles of shoes, such as wellies, slippers, sandals and crocs, in sizes that children can move in safely. Play the backing track for the song *One pair of shoes* several times, asking children to respond and dance wearing the different kinds of footwear. Do certain shoes make children want to dance differently? Is it difficult to dance in wellies? Is it easier to dance in bare feet or with shoes on?

ONLINE RESOURCES
Home learning

Story
The helpful elves

Audio
The shoemaker's piggy bank (song)
One pair of shoes (chant)
Midnight (song)
Presents for the elves (song)
One pair of shoes backing track
Impressions: III. To the point (listening)

Image
Match the person and the footwear

Notes

For additional resources, visit collins.co.uk/CPMEYFS/download
© 2021 HarperCollinsPublishers Ltd

OUR GROWING WORLD

Children love to grow things and a sunflower seed is often the first seed they plant.

Place a copy of Van Gogh's wonderful sunflower painting in a frame and display it on an easel, or use this similar image (see online resources). Ask children if they think the artist liked sunflowers. Do they think he grew the ones he painted?

Talk about being an artist and collect children's ideas of what an artist does. Some children may think artists only use paint, so talk about artists who work with different materials, e.g. sculptors, photographers, weavers, film-makers, etc. If you know an artist, perhaps someone who works in a different medium, e.g. a sculptor or cartoonist, invite them to come to your setting and work with the children.

ENHANCING CONTINUOUS PROVISION

Play dough
Make play dough as usual, but add a few drops of lavender oil or rose water to give a floral scent. Provide a variety of flower petals and leaves for the children to add to their dough.

Water
Collect flowers and leaves with the children. Encourage children to cut these up with scissors and add them to a tray of perfumed soapy water to make 'flower soup'. Have some bowls, jugs, spoons and pans to support children's play.

Sand
Add sunflower seeds, dried peas and beans to dry sand, and invite children to explore the mixture. Provide sieves and bowls for children to sift and collect the seeds and pulses. Introduce magnifying glasses for closer inspection.

Painting
Provide natural objects such as fir cones, conkers, conker cases, leaves, stones, pebbles, shells and 'slices' of small logs with trays of paints and paper sheets. Children can then use these materials in any creative way, e.g. painting the objects directly or dipping them in paint to use as printing tools.

Small world and construction
Introduce trays of grass, gravel, soil, sand and hay to the small world area to enhance children's play and encourage them to build farms and garden centres.

OUR GROWING WORLD

Role play
Turn your role play area into a garden centre by providing a tub of peat-free compost, various plant pots, water, watering cans, seed trays and seeds for children to explore activities associated with planting.

Creative design
Find as many different-sized photo frames as possible and remove the glass and backs. Provide plenty of natural resources, e.g. fir cones, conkers, conker cases, leaves, stones, flowers, pebbles, shells and 'slices' of small logs. Encourage children to create a collage to display in a frame – adding a sense of worth and importance to the work. You could also add an image of one of Andy Goldsworthy's land art works to inspire the children's creations. This activity can be replicated on a much larger scale in the outdoor area.

For additional resources, visit collins.co.uk/CPMEYFS/download
© 2021 HarperCollinsPublishers Ltd

Our growing world

MUSICAL LEARNING

Sunflower seeds

Sing or play the song, and invite children to join in with the three repeated lines in each verse and the clapped beats. Make simple shakers from small boxes part-filled with seeds or pulses (ideally use sunflower seeds to link to the song). Try to find transparent containers for the shakers so that children begin to understand that sounds occur when something moves. Once the verses are familiar, encourage children to substitute shaker sounds for the two clapped beats.

Growing up!

This is an echo song so model each line or use the recording for children to copy-sing. Every phrase is made up of 'stepping', or next-door notes, which will support children's 'pitch-matching'. The song has a rocking rhythm, so model rocking from side to side on the strong beat as you sing, and invite children to mirror your movements. Discuss children's heights and help them to arrange themselves in height order. Do they think they will ever be as tall as a tree?

SONG

Sunflower seeds

Melody: *If you're happy and you know it*

I can hold a tiny seed in my hand, [clap, clap]
I can hold a tiny seed in my hand, [clap, clap]
I can hold a tiny seed and I wonder what it needs!
I can hold a tiny seed in my hand. [clap, clap]

I can plant a tiny seed in the earth, [clap, clap]
I can plant a tiny seed in the earth, [clap, clap]
I can plant a tiny seed and I know just what it needs!
I can plant a tiny seed in the earth. [clap, clap]

I can see a tiny shoot start to grow, [clap, clap]
I can see a tiny shoot start to grow, [clap, clap]
I can see a tiny shoot and I know there'll be a root!
I can see a tiny shoot start to grow. [clap, clap]

I can see a yellow flower in the air, [clap, clap]
I can see a yellow flower in the air, [clap, clap]
I can see a yellow flower, and it's taller than a tower!
I can see a yellow flower in the air. [clap, clap]

I can hold a hundred seeds in my hand, [clap, clap]
I can hold a hundred seeds in my hand, [clap, clap]
I can hold a hundred seeds, they're what every
    gardener needs!
I can hold a hundred seeds in my hand. [clap, clap]

SONG

Growing up! 29

Leader:	Echo:
I'm growing tall.	I'm growing tall.
Tall as can be.	Tall as can be.
Tall as a house!	Tall as a house!
Tall as a tree!	Tall as a tree!
When will I stop	When will I stop
Growing so high?	Growing so high?
If I don't stop,	If I don't stop,
I'll touch the sky!	I'll touch the sky!

For additional resources, visit collins.co.uk/CPMEYFS/download
© 2021 HarperCollinsPublishers Ltd

33

Our growing world

ONLINE RESOURCES
Home learning

Audio
Sunflower seeds (song)
Growing up! (song)

Images
Sunflower heads
Growing sunflowers
Sunflowers in a vase

Notes

AGES 3-4

COMMUNICATION AND LANGUAGE

Fill a bag with items or images beginning with the letter 's', e.g. 'sunflower', 'spoon', 'snake', etc. Share them with the children and ask if they can think of other words beginning with this letter. Do any of the children's names begin with 'S'?

PERSONAL, SOCIAL AND EMOTIONAL DEVELOPMENT

Make a bucket full of kindness! Cut out pictures of sunflower heads (see online resources) and add a 'kind' message to each flower, e.g. 'Let someone else go first'; 'Listen carefully to your friend'; 'Say something nice to someone'; 'Share an activity with a friend', etc. Ask children to pick a sunflower and carry out the 'kind' action.

PHYSICAL DEVELOPMENT

If possible, use a real sunflower head for this activity, but if this is not possible, make a painted sunflower with children and put a pot containing sunflower seeds in the centre. Provide small bowls and tweezers and encourage children to extract the seeds and transfer them into the bowls.

LITERACY

Sing the song *Sunflower seeds* and when it is familiar, help children to identify the rhyming pairs: seed/need; shoot/root; flower/tower.

MATHEMATICS

Place six yellow paper cake cases in a bun tin and number them 1 to 6. Provide a small dish of sunflower seeds and ask the children to count the corresponding number of seeds into each paper case. Place two or three seeds in separate cases and mention "we have two in this case and three in that case", occasionally asking the children if they can recognise the number without counting.

UNDERSTANDING THE WORLD

Provide each child with a small container filled with peat-free compost and a sunflower seed. Encourage the children to plant and water their seeds, and nurture them (see online resources). As the seedlings grow, explain about the need to 'transplant' them into larger pots and, if the flowers need support, you can add sticks.

EXPRESSIVE ARTS AND DESIGN

In the creative area, place an image of Van Gogh's painting *Sunflowers* (or use the *Sunflowers in a vase* image in the online resources), or have some real sunflowers in a vase, to inspire children to paint their own version.

Our growing world

ONLINE RESOURCES
Home learning

Audio
Sunflower seeds (song)
Growing up! (song)

Image
Sunflowers in a vase

Templates
Sunflower and ladybird noughts and crosses
How to look after a sunflower seed

AGES 4-5

COMMUNICATION AND LANGUAGE

Take photographs of the plants and trees that grow in your outside area. Ask children to look carefully at these images and describe what they see. Work with a small group to support children as they try to work out where each photograph was taken.

PERSONAL, SOCIAL AND EMOTIONAL DEVELOPMENT

Ask children to think about how they have grown and changed since they were babies, e.g. how they have learnt to talk and walk. Encourage them to consider the things they like to do and the food they like to eat and discuss the fact that their choices may be different from their friends.

PHYSICAL DEVELOPMENT

Print and laminate a set of nine sunflowers and nine ladybirds (see online resources). In the outside area, support the children to chalk a giant 'noughts and crosses' grid. This activity can be played in pairs or teams to see who can complete the first full row of sunflowers or ladybirds.

LITERACY

Ask children to write a set of instructions for how to plant and look after a sunflower seed (see online resources).

MATHEMATICS

Print a copy of Van Gogh's painting *Sunflowers* (or use the *Sunflowers in a vase* image in the online resources). Invite children to look carefully at the painting and estimate how many flowers they think are in the vase before counting the actual number and writing down the number of sunflowers in the painting (scribe for children who need support). Use positional language to talk about the individual sunflowers, e.g. the smallest sunflower is at the bottom on its own.

UNDERSTANDING THE WORLD

Help children to fill a shallow tray with water. Provide safety knives and encourage children to cut the tops off carrots, beetroot and turnips and the bottoms off celery, onions and lettuces. Children then place these in the water tray to see if the vegetables start to regrow.

EXPRESSIVE ARTS AND DESIGN

Place a single sunflower in the creative area and encourage children to look at it very carefully and use their observational skills to paint or draw their own interpretation.

DO YOU SEE DINOSAURS?

Most children love dinosaurs and can tell you their complex names and characteristics. Dinosaurs provide a great opportunity to talk about creatures that are now extinct and to compare life when they ruled the earth, to life in the 21st century.

You could show the image (see online resources) or share it with children on a whiteboard, but it could be more engaging if you printed and mounted it on thin card to act as a backdrop to a 'Tuff' tray filled with grass, leaves, twigs and model dinosaurs. Talk with children about the different dinosaur species, where they lived and what they ate. Discuss carnivores, herbivores and omnivores and how we know so much about these creatures, even though they lived so long ago.

ENHANCING CONTINUOUS PROVISION

Play dough
Make brown-green play dough and provide plastic dinosaurs and different types of pasta for 'bones' and encourage children to imprint the shapes in the dough.

Water
The day before you need them, create 'dinosaur eggs'. Place small plastic dinosaurs individually into small plastic bags or balloons filled with water. Seal these securely and place in the freezer overnight. Add the frozen 'dinosaur eggs' to the water tray, minus their wrappings, so that children can observe how long they take to 'hatch'.

Sand
Place 'dinosaur bones' in the sand tray – these can be purchased online or made from salt-dough. Ask children to become archaeologists and use small trowels and paint brushes to unearth the bones. Provide magnifying glasses for a closer examination.

Small world and construction
Place a tray of green sand, pebbles, leaves, twigs, grass and plastic dinosaurs in the area, to encourage children to create a dinosaur's habitat.

Painting
Set out paper and trays of different coloured paints. Provide different plastic dinosaurs to be dipped in the paint for printing dinosaur footprints and shapes.

DO YOU SEE DINOSAURS?

Role play
Print out dinosaur shoe covers on card (see online resources) and use string or ribbon to attach them to children's shoes. Provide pieces of green and brown fabric, too, so that children can transform themselves into terrifying dinosaurs!

Creative design
Fill a 'Tuff' tray with soil, leaves, logs, fir cones and rocks for children to make into a dinosaur habitat.

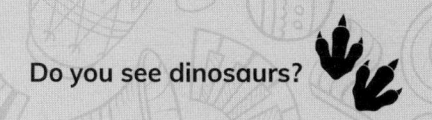

Do you see dinosaurs?

MUSICAL LEARNING

Dinosaur parade
Model singing the first line of the song and encourage children to join in with the echo response whilst swaying from side to side, plodding on their heavy dinosaur feet to the strong beat. Provide a range of recycled soundmakers, e.g. 'shakers', 'flappers' (large envelopes work well) and 'sploshers' (see online resources) for children to play after the question, 'Can you hear it roar?' Adapt the actions for the different dinosaurs in subsequent verses.

Tyrannosaurus rex
Model singing the song, encouraging the children to join in with the repeated line: 'It's Tyrannosaurus rex!'. The simple downward-stepping melody will help children 'pitch-match'. Explore making dinosaur sounds on different instruments and soundmakers to accompany these repeated lines.

Dance of the knights
Encourage the children to imagine they are dinosaurs (they might like to wear their dinosaur shoe covers in this activity – see Role play) and explore the music by:
- Plodding and stomping slowly with heavy bodies like a diplodocus, swaying slowly from side to side, stretching out one arm and hand to represent the dinosaur's neck and head. Model making your 'dinosaur' steps land on the strong beat (or pulse).
- Pounding around like a terrifying tyrannosaurus with strong leg movements and making fierce, snapping jaws with hands that open and slam shut.
- Flying like a pterodactyl, letting arms open and fold like wings, then soaring with arms outspread, moving up and down gliding smoothly through the air.

SONG

Dinosaur parade 31

Melody: *Old MacDonald*

Leader: Here comes a triceratops, thumping on the ground!
Echo: Here comes a triceratops, thumping on the ground!
Leader: It's a dinosaur! Can you hear it roar?
[DINOSAUR ROARING SOUNDS]
All: Here comes a triceratops, thumping on the ground!

Leader: Here comes Archaeopteryx, flying through the air!
Echo: Here comes Archaeopteryx, flying through the air!
Leader: It's a dinosaur! Can you see it soar?
[DINOSAUR SOARING SOUNDS]
All: Here comes Archaeopteryx, flying through the air!

Leader: Here comes Spinosaurus now, swimming through the waves!
Echo: Here comes Spinosaurus now, swimming through the waves!
Leader: It's a dinosaur! And it's on the shore!
[DINOSAUR SPLASHING SOUNDS]
All: Here comes Spinosaurus now, swimming through the waves!

POEM

Tyro the baby dinosaur 30

Tyro worries that she will never be as big and strong as her mum. (See page 54.)

SONG

Tyrannosaurus rex 32

Look out, ev'ryone, here he comes,
It's Tyrannosaurus rex!
His tail will swipe you off the ground,
It's Tyrannosaurus rex!
His jaws are huge and his teeth are too.
He's hungry and he'd like to swallow you!
It's Tyrannosaurus rex!

Look out, ev'ryone, here he comes,
It's Tyrannosaurus rex!
His tail will swipe you off the ground,
It's Tyrannosaurus rex!
His jaws are huge and his teeth are too.
He'll chomp you up and turn you into stew!
It's Tyrannosaurus rex!

LISTENING MUSIC

Sergei Prokofiev:
Dance of the knights (extract)
from the **Romeo and Juliet suite** 33

A piece for full orchestra in which string and brass instruments play melodies that move up and down in pitch to very strongly marked rhythms.

For additional resources, visit collins.co.uk/CPMEYFS/download
© 2021 HarperCollinsPublishers Ltd

Do you see dinosaurs?

ONLINE RESOURCES
Home learning

Poem
Tyro the baby dinosaur

Audio
Dinosaur parade (song)
Tyrannosaurus rex (song)
Dance of the knights (listening)

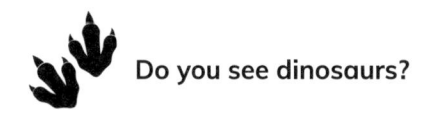

Templates
Dinosaur feet
Dinosaur shortbread recipe

AGES 3-4

COMMUNICATION AND LANGUAGE

Give each child a stick or short length of dowel – these could be painted green and decorated with a dinosaur sticker, if appropriate, to link to the theme. Ask children to explore the outdoor area, tapping as many different objects as they can find – upturned plant pots, the fence, doors, grass – listening to the sounds produced on each surface. If possible, record this exploration and share the recordings, talking about the differences between the sounds.

PERSONAL, SOCIAL AND EMOTIONAL DEVELOPMENT ⬇ 31

Sing *Dinosaur parade*, and after the line: 'Can you hear it roar?' ask children to take turns in making loud roaring sounds with their voices. Was anyone really scared by the roars?

PHYSICAL DEVELOPMENT ⬇

Create dinosaur 'feet' (see online resources) by covering empty tissue boxes with green-brown paper and gluing pasta 'claws' to the front. Use ribbon or string to tie them onto children's feet. Encourage children to stomp around in the outside area like giant dinosaurs!

LITERACY ⬇ 30

Share the poem *Tyro the baby dinosaur* encouraging children to join in when they can. Invite them to experiment with their voices, making roaring and squeaking sounds, as indicated in the text.

MATHEMATICS

Provide a selection of plastic dinosaurs in different sizes and a plentiful supply of counting blocks. Model stacking and counting the number of blocks needed to measure each dinosaur's height and invite children to join in. Use this approach and work together to find the tallest and shortest dinosaurs. Encourage children to then continue this activity independently.

UNDERSTANDING THE WORLD

Prepare a dinosaur hunt by hiding objects around the setting, e.g. dinosaur (pasta) 'teeth', dinosaur (salt-dough) 'bones', dinosaur (pebble) 'eggs', fossils and dinosaur footprints. Help children to make cardboard tube binoculars to assist them in their search!

EXPRESSIVE ARTS AND DESIGN ⬇

Make shortbread together (see online resources). If possible, arrange for every child to have their own bowl and set of ingredients. Model the mixing sequence, and encourage children to tackle the tasks of making dough and cutting out shapes independently. Offer children a selection of clean plastic dinosaur moulds to press into their dough to make dinosaur biscuits.

Do you see dinosaurs?

ONLINE RESOURCES
Home learning

Poem
Tyro the baby dinosaur

Audio
Dinosaur parade (song)
Tyrannosaurus rex (song)
Dance of the knights (listening)

Images
Dinosaur pictures
Reptile pictures

Templates
Dinosaur dice board game
Dinosaur action spinning wheel
Dinosaur shape

Notes

AGES 4-5

COMMUNICATION AND LANGUAGE

Say a dinosaur name and encourage the children to say and clap out each phoneme, then blend the phonemes together again. As they become more confident, ask individual children to choose a new dinosaur name to segment and blend independently.

PERSONAL, SOCIAL AND EMOTIONAL DEVELOPMENT

Ask children to help you to create a dinosaur game – this could be a board game with a dice (see online resources) or a game to be played outside. These game designers will need to identify resources and set the rules for other children to follow.

PHYSICAL DEVELOPMENT

Make a dinosaur action spinning wheel (see online resources): ask children to spin the wheel in turn and respond to the movements indicated by the arrow.

LITERACY

Show the children pictures of dinosaurs (see online resources) and ask children to select one, then say and write a caption for their chosen image.

MATHEMATICS

Cut dinosaur shapes out of green card (see online resources) and write a different number on each one. Provide clothes pegs and ask children to add pegs to each dinosaur card to match its number. As children progress, extend the activity by writing addition or subtraction sums on the cards.

UNDERSTANDING THE WORLD

Display the dinosaur pictures (see online resources), or read a non-fiction book about dinosaurs. Talk with children about past and present and focus on the time when dinosaurs lived on Earth, explaining that they have now become 'extinct'. Show photographs of different reptiles, e.g. gecko, Komodo dragon, crocodile (see online resources). Ask children if they think that these creatures might have 'evolved' from dinosaurs and give their reasons.

EXPRESSIVE ARTS AND DESIGN

Put out trays of green, brown, yellow and red paints with a selection of different-shaped leaves. Ask children to use the leaves, hands and fingers, to create their own dinosaur paintings.

For additional resources, visit collins.co.uk/CPMEYFS/download
© 2021 HarperCollinsPublishers Ltd

A SKY FULL OF COLOUR

Rainbows are some of the most beautiful and magical natural phenomena that we ever experience. Children should understand that rainbows appear when sun and rain occur at the same time, but to give the complex scientific explanation of rainbow formation is too advanced for young children.

Showing the short video of the beautiful rainbow (see online resources), with its amazing colours which fade quickly, will provide an opening for discussion and, hopefully, spark some interesting conversations and questions. It is also possible to create your own rainbow on a sunny day with a hosepipe!

ENHANCING CONTINUOUS PROVISION

A SKY FULL OF COLOUR

Play dough
Prepare play dough in the seven rainbow colours and place an image of a rainbow alongside (see online resources). Encourage children to explore the different colours of dough and to tell you what happens to the colour when you mix the doughs together.

Water
Fill empty washing-up liquid bottles with diluted paint. Encourage children to squirt this into water, asking them what happens to the colour of the water as different paints are added.

Sand
Place ribbons in each of the seven rainbow colours in the sand for children to find. Talk about rainbows as children are playing, and ask if they would like to make the ribbons they have found into a rainbow.

Small world and construction
Print and laminate an image of a rainbow (see online resources) and use this as a mat for small world play.

Painting
Collect several well-rinsed 'roll-on' deodorant bottles. Fill each one with a different rainbow colour shade of paint and encourage children to create their own roller rainbow pictures.

Role play
Collect scarves or pieces of fabric in rainbow colours and leave these in the role play area for children to use in their play.

Creative design
Collect sticks and twigs from the outside area or gather some during a walk. Provide strips of crêpe or tissue paper in each rainbow colour for children to attach to the sticks and twigs with tape or glue. Encourage children to use these rainbow streamers in dance.

For additional resources, visit collins.co.uk/CPMEYFS/download
© 2021 HarperCollinsPublishers Ltd

A sky full of colour

MUSICAL LEARNING

Colours shining
Model the song, inviting children to join in initially with the repeating lines: 'In the sky, in the sky', before tackling the whole song. This melody has an appealing skipping rhythm – encourage children to skip about freely, waving rainbow streamers made in continuous provision (Creative design).

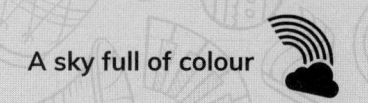

Look out for rainbows
Show an image of a rainbow (see online resources) to help singers remember the colour order as they sing. Make rainbow shakers using small clear plastic boxes: ask children to draw and colour small rainbow images to fit inside and add some coloured beads in rainbow colours to make the 'rattle'. Seal the shakers with brightly coloured tape and invite children to improvise accompaniments to the song.

If you have rainbow-coloured Boomwhackers or chime bars, model playing the rainbow colours in order: red, orange, yellow, green, blue, indigo, violet and ending with the smaller red one, to create a 'rainbow tune'. These eight notes form a 'scale' of next-door notes that goes up in pitch, getting higher step-by-step.

Ame no ki (Rain tree)
Explore the music by encouraging children to:
- Dance about as they flutter dancing fingers from high to low, representing lightly falling raindrops.
- Wave coloured streamers in large arcs in the air, making rainbow shapes.
- Make turning, twisting movements, trailing lightweight coloured scarves through the air, sweeping them high and low.

STORY
Danny's tasty rainbow ⬇ 34

Danny visits the greengrocer's shop and makes a fruit and vegetable rainbow. (See page 55.)

SONG
Colours shining ⬇ 35

Melody: *Here we go round the mulberry bush*

Colours shining in the sky,
In the sky, in the sky.
Colours shining in the sky
To make a beautiful rainbow!

Rain and sun will have to meet
In the sky, in the sky.
Rain and sun will have to meet
To make a beautiful rainbow!

Seven colours in the sky,
In the sky, in the sky.
Seven colours in the sky
To make a beautiful rainbow!

SONG
Look out for rainbows ⬇ 36

Raindrops fall, the sky is grey
But the sun's still out to play.
Rain and sun,
Sun and rain,
Make a rainbow shine for us again!

Look for red and orange,
Look for yellow, green and blue,
Indigo and
Violet too,
Make a rainbow shine for me and you!

LISTENING MUSIC
**Toru Takemitsu:
Ame no ki (Rain tree)** (extract) ⬇ 37

A really magical percussion piece for three people playing bells, marimbas and xylophone.

For additional resources, visit collins.co.uk/CPMEYFS/download
© 2021 HarperCollinsPublishers Ltd

A sky full of colour

ONLINE RESOURCES
Home learning

Story
Danny's tasty rainbow

Audio
Colours shining (song)
Look out for rainbows (song)
Ame no ki (listening)

Video
A sky full of colour video

Image
Outdoor image

Notes

AGES 3-4

COMMUNICATION AND LANGUAGE

Show *A sky full of colour* video (see online resources). Ask children if they've ever seen a rainbow and, if so, where they saw it. Share the myth that tells of a pot of gold waiting at the rainbow's end. Find out what they think about that!

PERSONAL, SOCIAL AND EMOTIONAL DEVELOPMENT

Make seven cardboard circles – one in each colour of the rainbow. Talk with children about the four key emotions: happiness, sadness, anger and excitement. Pass the cards to the children and ask them if any of the colours make children feel any of the emotions that you have discussed.

PHYSICAL DEVELOPMENT

Ask children to help you chalk a giant rainbow in the outdoor area, leaving spaces between the colours. Encourage children to jump through the rainbow landing in the spaces.

LITERACY

Share the story *Danny's tasty rainbow* and talk about the fruit, vegetables and flowers that Danny used to make his rainbow, or better still bring some in to show. Ask children to think of different fruit and vegetables they could have used instead, e.g. bananas instead of courgettes for 'yellow'.

MATHEMATICS

Fill a basket with a mixture of fruit and vegetables in rainbow colours and ask children to count all the items. Can they sort the items by colour? Can they separate the fruit and vegetables and count the numbers in each group? Can they correctly guess the number of oranges in the basket?

UNDERSTANDING THE WORLD

Ask children to each bring in a photograph that shows them in an outdoor location. Talk about the place, what the weather was like and whether there was a rainbow in the photograph. You could use the Outdoor image in the online resources for any children without their own photograph.

EXPRESSIVE ARTS AND DESIGN

Have a plentiful supply of pieces of rainbow-coloured tissue paper. Talk with children about the different colours and invite them to make their own pictures by sticking the tissue paper onto sheets of paper or cardboard rolls, giving them a choice of flat or curved surfaces.

A sky full of colour

ONLINE RESOURCES

Home learning

Story
Danny's tasty rainbow

Audio
Colours shining (song)
Look out for rainbows (song)
Ame no ki (listening)

Video
A sky full of colour video

Notes

AGES 4-5

COMMUNICATION AND LANGUAGE

Talk with children about the colours of the rainbow and ask them to think of real or nonsense rhyming words for some of the colours, e.g. red/bed, blue/shoe, green/bean... Can children use these words to make a poem?

PERSONAL, SOCIAL AND EMOTIONAL DEVELOPMENT

The rainbow has often been used as a symbol of hope. Watch A sky full of colour video (see online resources). Talk with children about how a rainbow makes them feel.

PHYSICAL DEVELOPMENT

Add streamers of rainbow-coloured crêpe paper or ribbons to short lengths of dowel. Encourage the children to move their rainbow streamers to music.

LITERACY   34

Share the story Danny's tasty rainbow. Ask children to write a shopping list of the fruit and vegetables that they enjoy eating.

MATHEMATICS

Count the number of colours in the rainbow. Number each from 1 to 7 and ask the children to find the corresponding number of coloured items in the setting.

UNDERSTANDING THE WORLD   36

Sing the song Look out for rainbows to remind the children of the colours of the rainbow, then talk with children about the weather conditions that are needed before a rainbow can appear in the sky.

EXPRESSIVE ARTS AND DESIGN

Ask children to help you make a large hand-print rainbow to display on the wall. Sketch a rainbow arc roughly on a large sheet of paper, marking each of the seven different bands. Fill trays with each rainbow colour of paint and ask the children to use their hands to print the seven different colours in order.

For additional resources, visit collins.co.uk/CPMEYFS/download
© 2021 HarperCollinsPublishers Ltd

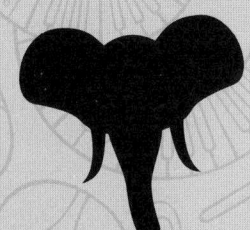

AMAZING AFRICAN ANIMALS

Display the image (see online resources). Of all the animals in the world, these amazing African animals are some of the most loved and the best known. This image includes a lion, leopard, rhino, elephant and buffalo – which are sometimes referred to as the 'Big Five'. Talk with children about the 'Big Five' and see if they can identify them in the image. Ask children why they think they are known as the 'Big Five'. Is it due to their power and strength or because they are the biggest, tallest, fastest animals in the world?

Talk about endangered animals and what we can do to help. Talk about the African national parks and wildlife reserves such as the Serengeti and the Masai Mara and other centres where endangered animals can live safely. You might like to discuss how Africa is a continent made up of lots of different countries.

ENHANCING CONTINUOUS PROVISION

Play dough
Make yellow and brown play dough and collect leaves and small sticks for children to add to the dough. Provide plastic African animals for children to press into the dough or to make footprints.

Sand
Add gold eco-glitter to the sand plus a large number of different-sized pebbles sprayed with gold paint. Provide jugs of water and panning-style basins and sieves for children to mine Ghanaian gold!

Water
Help children to create an African watering hole. Cover the bottom of the water tray with a small amount of water, add soil mixed with cornflour and encourage children to explore the mud with large twigs. They could add animals, pebbles, rocks and leaves, too.

Small world and construction
Share images of dwellings in African countries (see online resources). Place lentils in a 'Tuff' tray and add broccoli stems for trees. Provide sticks, straw, grass and other resources to make mud huts, bricks to make brick houses, or plastic African animals to make a wildlife park. Include pebbles and blue shiny paper (or a tray of water) for creating a watering hole.

Painting
Collect soil from the outside area with the children's help. Provide bowls and jugs of water, and invite children to mix water with the soil and paint with this liquid mud, using paintbrushes, twigs or parts of plants. You could help children to make their own leaf, twig and string brushes to create pictures.

AMAZING AFRICAN ANIMALS

Role play
Invite children to make housing structures such as mud huts or houses for role play (see online resources), e.g. use a pop-up tent with support walls made from painted corrugated card, and a roof made from a cone covered with straw. Cover cushions with fabrics from different African countries and make a small stick fire with a large cooking pot. Encourage children to identify other resources that they might like to add.

Creative design
Provide clay for children to explore. They could cover cylindrical cardboard containers to make mud huts to enhance their small world play, or use the clay to make bowls and plates for food – these could be dried, decorated and varnished then used in the role play area.

For additional resources, visit collins.co.uk/CPMEYFS/download
© 2021 HarperCollinsPublishers Ltd

Amazing African animals

MUSICAL LEARNING

Mangwane mpulele

This is a traditional African song from Botswana. The words mean, 'Aunty, open the door; the rain is pouring down on me', and provide a link with the story of Wiley, the lost wildebeest in *Searching in the Serengeti*. Enjoy listening to the recording and the instrumental accompaniment. The Sotho words: 'Mpulele ke nelwa ke pula' are sung frequently and will probably be the ones that children pick up most readily. This song has a gentle rocking rhythm so encourage children to respond with swaying movements as they listen.

Come to the Serengeti

Display the *Amazing African animals* image (see online resources) and discuss the animals of the Serengeti, especially those mentioned in the song: lion, elephant and monkey. Print images of some of the instruments that provide the accompaniment (see online resources). Play the recording and enjoy listening to the interesting percussion sounds played on the frog, rainstick and basket rattle. Encourage children to join in with some lines as they become familiar, particularly the recurring lines: 'Come to the Serengeti, where all the animals play' and 'We'll all have some fun!'. Accompany your singing by playing a guiro or other 'scraper' percussion instrument (or create a similar sound effect by running a stick along a ridged plastic bottle).

STORY
Searching in the Serengeti — 38

A little wildebeest is lost, but a young hippo and a lion cub save the day. (See page 55.)

SONG

Mangwane mpulele — 39

Mangwane mpulele ke nelwa ke pula,
Mangwane mpulele ke nelwa ke pula,
Mangwane mpulele ke nelwa ke pula,
Mangwane mpulele ke nelwa ke pula.

Le fa dile pedi le fa dile tharonka nyala mosadi,
Le fa dile pedi le fa dile tharonka nyala mosadi,
Le fa dile pedi le fa dile tharonka nyala mosadi,
Le fa dile pedi le fa dile tharonka nyala mosadi.

Mpulele, mpulele, mpulele ke nelwa ke pula,
Mpulele, mpulele, mpulele ke nelwa ke pula,
Mpulele, mpulele, mpulele ke nelwa ke pula,
Mpulele, mpulele, mpulele ke nelwa ke pula.

SONG

Come to the Serengeti — 40

Come to the Serengeti,
Who's out in the grasslands today?
Come to the Serengeti,
Where all the animals play!

Can you see over there,
A lion in the sun?
When it gets colder
We'll all have some fun!

Come to the Serengeti,
Who's out in the grasslands today?
Come to the Serengeti,
Where all the animals play!

Can you see over there,
An elephant in the sun?
When they spray us with water
We'll all have some fun!

Come to the Serengeti,
Who's out in the grasslands today?
Come to the Serengeti,
Where all the animals play!

Can you see over there,
A monkey in the sun?
When they swing in the trees
We'll all have some fun!

Come to the Serengeti,
Who's out in the grasslands today?
Come to the Serengeti,
Where all the animals play! They play!

For additional resources, visit collins.co.uk/CPMEYFS/download
© 2021 HarperCollinsPublishers Ltd

Amazing African animals

ONLINE RESOURCES
Home learning

Story
Searching in the Serengeti

Audio
Mangwane mpulele (song)
Come to the Serengeti (song)

Images
African animals and their babies
Traditional Samburu women in Kenya

Template
Animal faces

Notes

AGES 3-4

COMMUNICATION AND LANGUAGE

Share the story *Searching in the Serengeti* to set the scene. Hide several African animal models in the outside area. Write clues and read these out to children to help them identify each animal and find its hiding place. Once the animals have been found, ask children to choose new hiding places and then encourage them to help you write fresh clues for others to use.

PERSONAL, SOCIAL AND EMOTIONAL DEVELOPMENT

Ask children why they think lions roar – is it because they are happy, frightened, hungry or cross? Ask children to make a roaring sound like a lion. How does that make them feel?

PHYSICAL DEVELOPMENT

Play the game 'Sleeping lions'. Ask children to lie down on the floor and pretend that they are sleeping lions. Choose two of the children to be game wardens and encourage them to talk to the lions and try to make them laugh. If the sleeping lions move, they become game wardens, too. The winner is the last sleeping lion to wake up.

LITERACY

Sing the song *Come to the Serengeti* then talk with the children about the animals mentioned in the song. Ask children to pretend to be one of those animals by moving and making appropriate animal sounds.

MATHEMATICS

Ask children to help you create an animal face, e.g. monkey, giraffe, zebra or elephant – avoid carnivores, such as lions (use the face templates provided online if you wish). Stick the face onto a strong cardboard box and cut out a hole for the mouth. Find or make items to represent appropriate foods, e.g. for a monkey, cut out yellow cardboard bananas or represent bananas with yellow Lego bricks. Invite the children to take turns throwing a large dice, and to feed the animal the corresponding number of food items.

UNDERSTANDING THE WORLD

Print out the photos of the African animals and their babies (see online resources) and ask children to match the adult animals with their offspring. Talk with children about where the animals live.

EXPRESSIVE ARTS AND DESIGN

Show the picture of traditional Samburu women in Kenya (see online resources) to inspire children to a make their own necklaces. Use the rim of a paper plate, trimmed to the size of each child's neck and provide paint, glue, tissue paper and coloured pasta for children to make beads and decorations, as they wish.

Amazing African animals

ONLINE RESOURCES

Home learning

Story
Searching in the Serengeti

Audio
Mangwane mpulele (song)
Come to the Serengeti (song)

Video
Serengeti video

Images
Mask on sale in Kenya
Animal fur

Notes

AGES 4-5

COMMUNICATION AND LANGUAGE

Write the names of various African animals on pieces of card and hide these in the learning environment. Help the children to make binoculars by joining two cardboard tubes together lengthways and adding a length of string so that the binoculars can hang round children's necks. Encourage children to search for the cards with their binoculars and to try to sound out the letters in order to identify the animals' names.

PERSONAL, SOCIAL AND EMOTIONAL DEVELOPMENT

Display the image of a mask on sale in Kenya (see online resources). Ask the children to tell you how the mask makes them feel... is it a bit scary? Discuss with children how masks can have religious meanings and can also represent animals or the spirits of ancestors.

PHYSICAL DEVELOPMENT

Ask two children to create an 'elephant bridge' by facing each other and joining their 'trunks' (arms). Encourage other children to dance under the bridge in turn.

LITERACY

Share the story Searching in the Serengeti. Talk about the different animals and ask children what they think it would be like to live in that part of Africa. Invite children to write a letter to one of the characters, telling them which part of the story they liked best, or to draw a picture of their impression of the Serengeti.

MATHEMATICS

Conduct research with the children to find the average height of three African animals, e.g. a giraffe, an elephant and a lion. Help children to measure the height of the three animals on the ground in the outside area, using a metre ruler and string. Then, using the string as a guide, ask children to chalk an outline of each animal to show its true height.

UNDERSTANDING THE WORLD

Show a video of wildebeest travelling across the Serengeti plains (see online resources) and talk with children about what life is like for these animals. Encourage children to think about the differences between the Serengeti and where they live.

EXPRESSIVE ARTS AND DESIGN

Print out some examples of animal fur, e.g. leopard, zebra, cheetah and giraffe (see online resources). Provide children with different coloured paints, paintbrushes, sponges and other paint 'applicators' and invite them to create their own patterns, inspired by the animals' pelts.

UNDER THE SEA

Support the introduction of this image by filling a seaside bucket with shells and water. Ask children if they have visited the seaside. Have they put their feet in the sea?

Talk with the children about seas and oceans, e.g. about seawater being salty and about waves and tides. Explain that the Earth's surface is largely covered by sea and that the seas and oceans are very deep in places and are home to some incredible creatures and plants.

ENHANCING CONTINUOUS PROVISION

Play dough
Make blue, green and white play dough and roll this together for a marbled effect. Provide pots of 'Sea life' confetti along with any sea-related resources for children to add to or press into their dough.

Water
Add blue-green food colouring to the water tray to represent the sea and provide small plastic bottles for children to use as boats and submarines. Talk with children about what the submarine passengers would see under the ocean. You could add some of the resources from the sand tray.

Sand
Place a collection of different sea creatures in the sand tray – these might be plastic, wooden or even real dried skeletons of marine life, e.g. seahorses or cuttlefish bones. Add green ribbons for seaweed and include as many natural objects as possible, e.g. shells, sponges, pebbles and driftwood to support children's play.

Small world and construction
Encourage children to build an 'aquarium' using any junk modelling or construction materials. Print off pictures of different sea creatures (see online resources) for the children to cut out and place or suspend in their aquarium – some children may prefer to draw their own pictures.

Painting
Pour green, blue and white paint onto a large tray, or directly onto the table. Encourage children to use their fingers to make waves in the paint, mixing the colours together. Take prints of the 'swirls' created using a large piece of paper, and when these are dry, invite children to add drawings of sea creatures.

UNDER THE SEA

Role play
Find a large piece of blue-green fabric to represent the sea and place this on the floor. On the top, place containers that are large enough for the children to sit in to represent boats or rafts, e.g. empty water trays, baby baths or cardboard boxes.

Creative design
Collect pebbles and shells and place these in the creative area, providing adhesive wobbly eyes, pieces of coloured paper and sticky tape so that children can create weird and wonderful sea creatures.

For additional resources, visit collins.co.uk/CPMEYFS/download
© 2021 HarperCollinsPublishers Ltd

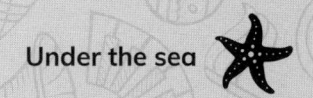

Under the sea

MUSICAL LEARNING

Sea creatures
Sing the song or listen to the recording a few times. Once the song pattern is familiar, ask children to make up actions for 'whoosh', 'swish', 'snap' and 'wriggle' – some children may choose soundmakers to play on these action words.

The sea is stuck in a shell
Explain the story behind the song before singing it. Encourage children to join in with the repeating line: 'But can the sea get out?' then, as the song becomes more familiar, try the longer final line: 'It will always keep splashing and crashing and bashing about!'. You could help children to make 'sploshers' for sea sounds to accompany the song (see online resources).

Aquarium
Encourage the children to imagine they are different sea creatures or sea life as they explore the music through movement, e.g.
- Being an octopus, with curling fingers and softly moving arms that wave about in all directions.
- Floating like a jellyfish, bobbing and turning gently in the water with fingers wiggling like tentacles.
- Being a shoal of little fish, following a leader, taking little steps and weaving round the space in different directions.
- Scuttling sideways like a crab, stopping and looking about, checking for predators.
- Drifting like seaweed, standing on the spot with arms outstretched and bodies swaying slowly in all directions.

STORY
Seashells for Serena ⬇ 41

A little mermaid decides to make a birthday present for her sister. (See page 53.)

SONG
Sea creatures ⬇ 42

Melody: *Baa baa black sheep*

(The verses are dedicated alternately to male and female characters, but if children find this too confusing, sing either 'he/his' or 'she/her' throughout for one performance and then swap on another occasion.)

In the ocean,
In the wavy sea,
Watch a big whale
Swim past me!
Whoosh! goes the big whale,
Whoosh! goes he,
Whoosh! goes the hungry whale,
He wants his tea!

In the ocean,
In the wavy sea,
Watch a big squid
Swim past me!
Swish! goes the big squid
Swish! goes she,
Swish! goes the hungry squid,
She wants her tea!

In the ocean,
In the wavy sea,
Watch a big shark
Swim past me!
Snap! goes the big shark
Snap! goes he,
Snap! goes the hungry shark,
He wants his tea!

In the ocean,
In the wavy sea,
Watch a big eel
Swim past me!
Wriggle! goes the big eel
Wriggle! goes she,
Wriggle! goes the hungry eel,
She wants her tea!

LISTENING MUSIC
Camille Saint-Saëns: Aquarium from **The carnival of the animals** ⬇ 44

A gently rippling melody is played by the flute, accompanied by strings and piano.

SONG
The sea is stuck in a shell ⬇ 43

The sea is stuck in a shell,
I hear it clear as a bell.
The sea is splashing about,
But can the sea get out?

I found the shell by the pier
And put it up to my ear.
The sea was splashing about,
But can the sea get out?

When I am far from the sea,
My shell plays music for me.
The sea can never get out!
It will always keep splashing and
  crashing and bashing about!

For additional resources, visit collins.co.uk/CPMEYFS/download
© 2021 HarperCollinsPublishers Ltd

49

Under the sea

ONLINE RESOURCES

Home learning

Story
Seashells for Serena

Audio
Sea creatures (song)
The sea is stuck in a shell (song)
Aquarium (listening)

Notes

AGES 3-4

COMMUNICATION AND LANGUAGE

Talk with children about the sea. Ask if they have ever visited the seaside, dipped their feet in the sea, listened to the waves splashing or held a large seashell to their ear to hear the sea. Encourage children who have not visited the sea to ask their peers questions about what the sea was like and to listen carefully to their answers.

PERSONAL, SOCIAL AND EMOTIONAL DEVELOPMENT ⬇ 41

Read the story *Seashells for Serena* and ask children what they think it would be like to live under the sea. Would they like living there? Would they enjoy being a mermaid or merman and swimming with sea creatures? What would they miss about life on land?

PHYSICAL DEVELOPMENT

Ask children to run around the outside area and when you call out the name of a sea creature they should stop, stand on the spot and make the shape or movement of that creature.

LITERACY ⬇ 42

Sing the song *Sea creatures*, and talk about the different fish and mammals listed in the lyrics. Ask children if they can think of any words that rhyme with the sea creatures in the song, e.g. 'whale' – 'snail', 'shark' – 'dark', 'eel' – 'seal'.

MATHEMATICS

Cut out paper fish shapes in different colours and in three different sizes; hide these around the learning environment. Send children on a 'fish hunt'. When all the fish have been found, ask children to group them by size, then count up the numbers of fish of each colour and finally find the total of all the fish.

UNDERSTANDING THE WORLD

Place natural objects such as shells, stones, sea urchin cases, driftwood and dried seaweed in the sand tray. As children play, encourage them to observe the objects closely and talk about the places where they would find them. Offer magnifying glasses and ask children to tell you what they see.

EXPRESSIVE ARTS AND DESIGN

Cut out fish shapes from thick fabric, such as felt. Encourage children to dip these fabric shapes into trays of paint and make prints on paper. Some children may prefer to apply paint directly onto the surface of the fabric and then press-print onto the paper.

Under the sea

AGES 4-5

ONLINE RESOURCES

Home learning

Story
Seashells for Serena

Audio
Sea creatures (song)
The sea is stuck in a shell (song)
Aquarium (listening)

Image
Lifeboats

Notes

COMMUNICATION AND LANGUAGE 43

Sing the song *The sea is stuck in a shell* and encourage children to tell you the story told in the lyrics. Acquire a large seashell. Invite children to hold the seashell to their ear and tell you what they hear. Can they hear the sea or another sound? Ask them how they think the sound gets into the shell. Enjoy the rhyming words in the lyrics that describe the sea: 'bashing', 'crashing', 'splashing'… Can children think of any more rhymes, e.g. dashing, mashing, smashing, flashing?

PERSONAL, SOCIAL AND EMOTIONAL DEVELOPMENT

Talk about the sea and safety: remind children that sometimes water can be very dangerous. Discuss ways of keeping safe when near water. Tell children about lifeboat stations; show images of lifeboats (see online resources) and describe how the crews help people who get into trouble.

PHYSICAL DEVELOPMENT

Create an 'Under the sea' obstacle course for children to complete before being caught in a fishing net, e.g. a piece of blue-green fabric to jump over, shells in a container to lay out in a line, paper fish to stick on a fishing rod, a sign saying 'eight jumps for each octopus tentacle', a tyre to climb over like a rock…

LITERACY 41

Listen to the story *Seashells for Serena*. Can children think of a reason why Octavia managed to collect so many shells? Ask the children to draw a labelled design for something that Serena could make with the leftover shells.

MATHEMATICS

Provide a bucket containing four kinds of 'sea' materials, e.g. shells, pebbles, cut-out paper fish and pieces of driftwood. Invite children to sort the contents into four empty buckets positioned round the edge of the chosen area. Ask children to record the number of items in each bucket. They could add up the contents of two buckets to find out how many shells and pebbles there are added altogether, recording these answers, too.

UNDERSTANDING THE WORLD

Have four containers filled with sand. Add a different liquid to each one, e.g. washing-up liquid, water, oil and hair conditioner. Ask children to investigate and discover what happens to sand when it is mixed with the different liquids. How does the sand feel different?

EXPRESSIVE ARTS AND DESIGN

Place sand, shells, sea life confetti, tissue paper, etc. in the creative area for children to make an 'Under the sea' collage.

STORIES AND POEMS

Zigi bounces to Mars

Zigi was up very, very early and when he opened his curtains, he could see a few twinkly stars shining in the sky. He'd woken up because he was planning a trip to Mars. He'd heard that Mars was called the 'red planet', so he pulled out his new red T-shirt and put on his favourite red trainers. Zigi decided he would make the journey on his space hopper, which was red, too. The space hopper had belonged to his two older brothers and some of the bounce had disappeared, but it was Zigi's absolute favourite toy.

He took three chocolate chip cookies for his breakfast and went out into the garden. It was dark and looked quite different in the moonlight. Zigi did some bouncing practice – he knew he'd need a really good bounce to launch himself into the sky. After a few goes, he made a huge effort and felt himself leaving the ground.

He bounced over the treetops, over the rooftops and past the church spire, up and up and up. He thought he ought to eat one of his biscuits in case it was a long journey, so he let go of one handle very carefully and munched one chocolate chip cookie. Zigi could no longer see any buildings below him. The stars seemed to get brighter and it got colder… he chewed another cookie.

Suddenly he found himself bouncing on the ground again, but it wasn't his garden; it was a big empty place and really dusty. "I think I'm on Mars!" said Zigi, and he got off the space hopper to explore. He looked round but there was nothing to see but rocks. He was just going to eat his third cookie when he saw another space hopper bouncing towards him, and another and another and another: they were bright green and made funny squeaking noises, but no one was riding them! Zigi got on his hopper again and they all raced round together, bouncing over the rocks, setting up dust clouds and having a really good time.

After a while, Zigi felt quite dizzy and hungry too. He stopped and his new friends stopped as well, and then they waved their hopper handles and bounced away. "That was fun," said Zigi, "but I don't think three biscuits is enough breakfast for someone who's nearly five… I think I'll go back home for some proper food!" He made one huge bounce and left the ground. Zigi spun round and round and twirled about in the sky, and then landed by his own back door. He could smell toast and beans and fried tomatoes and went inside.

"Hello," said Mum, "you are extremely dusty… have you been rolling in the flower beds?" "No," said Zigi, "I've been space-hopping on Mars with my new green friends!" "Oh," said Mum, "did they give you breakfast?" "No," said Zigi, "I thought I'd come back when my cookies ran out!" "Good plan," said Mum, "but go and wash your dusty face while I find something for a hungry space traveller – are your friends having breakfast with us today?" "Not today," said Zigi, "I'm going to eat it all myself… space-hopping makes you very hungry!"

Let's find treasure

Mr. Ahmed closed the book. Tiffany said, "Oh read it again, please! I really like it when you do the Captain's voice!" "And the bit about the monkeys is really funny!" added Isaac. Everyone giggled and so did Mr. Ahmed. Then he said, "I've read the story twice now and I think it's time for you to choose your activities – the story might give you some ideas."

Some children went to the sand tray. They piled up the sand to make a huge island then buried bits of treasure, poking stones and shells into the sand with their fingers. A few children painted pirate ships sailing on a deep blue sea. But Tiffany and Isaac wandered over to the role play area. Tiffany tipped out the basket of dressing-up clothes. "Look!" she said, "Here's a squashy hat and an eyepatch, so you can be the captain." Isaac was really pleased and said, "Listen 'ere, me 'earties," just like Captain Barney in the story. Tiffany laughed and tied a skull and crossbones scarf round her waist. "I can be your crew," she said. "But only if you do as you're told and find me some treasure!" commanded Captain Isaac! "Right, Captain!" she said, saluting him, then skipped off to find some treasure.

Tiffany found five fir cones, three coins and two Lego bricks and put them in a box. She went back to find Isaac balancing a toy monkey on the window ledge. "That looks good," said Tiffany, showing off her treasure. "Oh," said Isaac with a frown, "that's not the same as the treasure in the story. Do you remember? The monkeys threw coconuts at the crew and so the cook made coconut pie and coconut milkshake for supper. The treasure was something they could eat and drink!" "Well, I can't get that sort of treasure, can I?" she said crossly and folded her arms. "I don't think I want to be in this game any more!"

Just as Tiffany was about to walk off in a grumpy huff, Mr. Ahmed called out, "Snack time, everyone." Tiffany got to the tray first. There were slices of apple and oranges but there was also a new kind of fruit that they hadn't had before – it was white and it looked hard. "What's that?" she asked. "Can't you guess?" said Mr. Ahmed. "These fruits grow high up on trees in hot countries and monkeys are very good at throwing them at pirates!" "Coconuts!" laughed Isaac, who'd come to join Tiffany. "No," said Tiffany, forgetting her grumpy mood, "it's treasure!"

Stories and poems

Seashells for Serena [41]

In the blue-green sea that surrounds a tiny island, you might just be lucky enough to catch a glimpse of a silvery fishtail weaving in and out of the coral reef. But this is no fish! This is Serena – a mermaid – and she's searching for treasure... not the treasure that pirates get excited about; Serena is looking for shells – tiny, pearly, coloured shells. Her big sister has a birthday very soon and a present has to be found! There are no shops on the seabed, so Serena decides to make her sister a shell necklace.

The mermaid has been searching for hours but her basket isn't nearly full enough. Suddenly she sees her friend, Octavia, a pretty little octopus, who waves at Serena with all of her eight tentacles.

"Hi, Octavia," says Serena, "I'm so pleased to see you – I need some help and you're the perfect friend to ask!" The mermaid explains about the birthday and the necklace... "With your eight tentacles you could pick up heaps of shells really quickly. Please will you help me?"

Octavia propels herself through the sea like a rocket, collecting shells from the nooks and crannies along the seabed. She travels so quickly that she wakes a shoal of triggerfish dozing in the reef, and they dart to and fro, grumbling angrily about their disturbed nap. In a few minutes, the little octopus comes back with a pile of shells, filling the basket to the brim. "Thank you, Octavia, that's wonderful – you saved the day!" says Serena, and with a flick of her silvery tail, she swims off with her treasure.

The best shells are soon threaded onto a thin piece of seaweed and Serena's big sister is delighted with her present. "That's good," said Serena, "because you might get a shell bracelet and tiara next year – I have so many shells left over!"

My snowman [15]

It snowed yesterday.
The garden looked strange
But I ran out to play.

What would I do?
Build something huge,
But the snow filled my shoe!

"A snowman," I said,
"As tall as a tree
With a big snowball head."

He wasn't a tree,
My man made of snow,
He was small like me.

A scarf and a hat
And a carroty nose.
We all laughed at that!

But the sun shone today
On a snow ghost.
He was melting away...

Ai Lin cooks chow mein [19]

Ai Lin is five years old and she lives with her family in London. Her granny cooks all the food and her meals are delicious. Ai Lin always watches her granny cook supper. She stands with her chin just resting on the worktop and asks lots of questions: "Why does garlic smell so strong?... Why is ginger knobbly?... Why do mushrooms have stalks?" Granny smiles and tells her granddaughter all the answers.

One evening, Granny is preparing chow mein, Ai Lin's favourite. "Can I help, please, Granny?" Ai Lin asks. "Of course," replies Granny, "but we need you to be higher up – let's find you a tall stool and then you can do some of the work." Ai Lin was soon ready, sitting on a stool, with clean hands, an apron round her waist and a big grin – this was going to be fun!

Granny put out all the ingredients and told Ai Lin the names as she pointed to each one: oyster sauce, soy sauce and special chilli sauce... "That's a lot of bottles, Granny!" said Ai Lin. ...Garlic, ginger, oil, pak choy... "What's that, Granny?" "It's a special Chinese white cabbage." ...Shiitake mushrooms, bean sprouts and pan-fried noodles. "Wow, all that to make chow mein!" said Ai Lin, amazed at all the different ingredients spread out on the worktop.

"Now," said Granny, "first of all, I'm going to slice the mushrooms and pak choy. Next, I'm going to put some of the three sauces in a bowl and you're going to whisk them with this cook's chopstick, stirring fast to mix them up." While Ai Lin stirred, Granny put oil in a pan and after a minute, she added the noodles with the garlic and ginger – the mixture sizzled and smelt wonderful. Ai Lin watched from the safety of her stool as the chopped mushrooms and pak choy leaves were added to the hot pan. The smells just got better and better! Last of all, Granny added the sauces that Ai Lin had stirred so carefully, and the bean sprouts.

"Quickly, Ai Lin," said Granny, "call everyone to the table, this food needs eating NOW while it's hot!" Ai Lin called her family and soon they were tucking into chow mein with other tasty dishes that Granny had made earlier. Ai Lin was given a round of applause for being a splendid cooking assistant and she felt very proud.

"Tomorrow," said Granny, "you can help me make dim sum!" Ai Lin grinned – she would have a lot to tell her teacher tomorrow!

Stories and poems

The helpful elves

The shoemaker shook the piggy bank. He sighed and then shook his head. "We've no money at all!" he said with another sigh, "I've cut out the leather pieces for one last pair of shoes and I don't know what will happen after that!"

"It's nearly midnight," said his wife, "I think we should go to bed and you should try to stop worrying. You need sleep if you're going to finish those shoes first thing in the morning!"

They trudged up the stairs and got into bed just as the clock struck twelve. Soon they were both snoring.

The downstairs window slid open with a little creak and two little elves slipped inside and jumped up onto the shoemaker's workbench. They were no taller than a milk jug, with pointed ears and tiny pointed caps on their heads, but their clothes were ragged and patched and their tiny feet were bare.

"Come on," said Peri to Keri, "let's get started! Everything's been left ready for us to do our work! Look, there's leather, thread, needles, glue, hammers and nails. This will be an easy job!"

The elves started to sew the pieces together. Their needles flew in and out of the leather so quickly that you could hardly see the thread moving. Soon they had hammered the soles and heels and before you could say 'magic shoes', they had finished. The shoes were lovely. They gleamed with silver buckles and looked very smart! Keri grabbed his brother's hands and they jiggled and giggled as they danced round and round the shoes. Suddenly Peri stopped and said, "It's nearly morning! We must go before the shoemaker comes down. He'll be so surprised when he sees what we've done!" Keri nodded and they slipped out quietly through the window.

Next morning, when the shoemaker saw the shoes, he rubbed his eyes ...he rubbed them again – he just couldn't believe what he saw. "Look!" he said to his wife, "see the tiny dainty stitches! I can't stitch like that, it must be magic! Who could have made these wonderful shoes?" Bursting with excitement, he put them in the shop window and in five minutes they had been sold for a very good price. The silver coins jingled sweetly when he popped them into the piggy bank.

"I have enough money to buy leather for two pairs of shoes," said the shoemaker. "I shall leave the cut pieces out tonight and see what happens." And that's what they did.

In the morning there were two pairs of beautiful shoes sitting on the workbench and, just like the day before, they sold immediately. Even after buying leather for three pairs of shoes, the piggy bank still jingled sweetly and sounded very full.

The shoemaker's wife said, "Let's stay up tonight to see who's making the shoes. Whoever it is has made us rich and we ought to know who our helpers are, so that we can say, "Thank you." So, at midnight, they didn't go to bed; the shoemaker and his wife hid behind the curtain and watched as Keri and Peri arrived and made three pairs of beautiful shoes in no time at all. When the elves left, the shoemaker and his wife looked at each other in amazement... the elves were so tiny... their hands were so skilful... and their clothes were so shabby!

"I shall spend tomorrow making them shirts, trousers and jackets," said the shoemaker's wife. "And I shall make them leather shoes for their poor little bare feet!" said the shoemaker with a big smile.

The next night when the elves arrived, the workbench was empty except for two sets of tiny clothes and two pairs of tiny leather shoes. The shoemaker and his wife watched from their hiding place as Peri and Keri tried on their new outfits. The elves danced and pranced, they jiggled and giggled, and finally they left through the window.

The elves didn't return, but the shoemaker was never poor again. His shoes sold well and the piggy bank always jingled sweetly when he shook it.

Tyro the baby dinosaur

Tyro was a baby,
A Tyrannosaurus rex!
She wanted to be scary,
She really did her best!
But her feet were only little
And her tail was very weak,
And instead of making roaring sounds
She only made a squeak!

Tyro eyed her family,
They all looked tall and strong.
Her mum was like a monster
And her tail was tough and long.
"I'll never be like Mum", she wept,
"I'll never be that grand,
I'll always be the baby
In our dinosaur land."

Tyro's dad was watching,
He saw that she was glum.
He said, "Come over here, love,
Let's talk about your mum."
He opened up the album
Of photos from the past
And when he turned to one page
Young Tyro laughed and laughed.

For there was Tyro's mother,
A baby – two days old.
She wasn't huge and powerful,
She wasn't fierce and bold.
"You see," said Dad, "we all start out
As babies just like you,
But one day, little Tyro,
You'll be a monster, too!"

Stories and poems

Danny's tasty rainbow 34

Danny loved spending Saturdays with his aunty and uncle. They lived in a flat in the high street above Mr. Tomkins' greengrocer's shop. Whenever Danny went to visit, he'd gaze at all the fruit and vegetables set out in boxes at the front of the shop. Mr. Tomkins was his friend and always gave him a piece of fruit to eat.

One Saturday, Aunty Pat had a meeting and couldn't play games with him. Danny was getting bored, so his uncle said: "Let's pop down to the shop and see Mr. Tomkins, he might let you help out." Danny thought this was a great idea, so he and his uncle went downstairs and he was very pleased when the greengrocer said he could spend the afternoon in the shop. There weren't many customers that day, so Danny couldn't do much helping, but as he was tidying up a pile of old newspapers, he saw a big picture of a rainbow. "Look, Mr. Tomkins, isn't that great! I wish I could paint one like that!" "Well, I've no paints, Danny, but I do have plenty of coloured fruit and veg... would that do?"

Danny thought this was just the best idea ever! He started by making a curved line of red strawberries on the counter. Underneath these he added a row of little oranges, and after that he chose some yellow courgettes. He had to ask Mr. Tomkins what they were called because he'd never had those at home. Danny knew it was green next, so he chose some chillies; he recognised these because his mum used them in her cooking, but blue was going to be tricky – no blue fruit or vegetables to be seen anywhere. But, Mr. Tomkins had some blue delphiniums standing in a bucket in the corner, so Danny made a row of blue flowers – they looked lovely next to the chillies. The rainbow arch was looking very grand now. Mr. Tomkins helped with the last two colours – they decided on bluey-purple grapes for indigo and small shiny vegetables called 'aubergines' for violet – that was another new vegetable name to learn. Danny was delighted with his rainbow: Mr. Tomkins took a photo and said he'd put it in the shop window for all his customers to see.

Just then, Danny's uncle appeared in the shop and said that Aunty Pat was back from her meeting. Uncle loved the rainbow and was very impressed that Danny knew the words, 'courgettes' and 'aubergines'. He said: "I'm cooking supper tonight and I've got a new vegetarian recipe book to try out, so let's use those chillies, aubergines and courgettes and cook up something tasty!" So they did, and that evening they had a delicious veggie stew with Mr. Tomkins' new potatoes and some of Danny's rainbow strawberries for pudding.

Searching in the Serengeti 38

In East Africa, Wiley the Wildebeest and his family were looking for a new home for the summer. They walked all day and all night to find the perfect place to live. As they walked, Wiley heard a howling noise in the distance. He was curious and went to investigate what it could be. He ventured across the river and up the hill, where he saw two scary-looking jackals with sharp teeth and sharp claws and covered in dirt and dust. These hungry jackals were scavenging for their next meal. They noticed Wiley straight away, and started tiptoeing towards him. Wiley ran away as fast as he could! But, when he made it back, his family had gone!

Wiley was all alone and it was raining hard. He was wet and miserable. He spotted a small cave and decided to go there to hide from the jackals. As he got closer, he saw a hippo about his size blocking the door. "Please let me in," said Wiley. "I want to hide from those jackals." "Of course!" said the hippo, and she moved to let Wiley in. "Hello, I'm Hanifah" said the hippo, "I'm hiding from the jackals too. Let's stay here tonight – then will you help me get back to the watering hole tomorrow?" The two spent the night together, comforted by the familiar sound of the croaking crickets, and took turns at sleeping and keeping watch.

As the sun rose, the light spread across the land of the Serengeti showing them the wonders of their home. The birds were singing the loveliest songs and the bees were buzzing in the whispers of the wind. They discovered a dirt road and followed it. Suddenly a loud "ROARRR" broke the silence! Out popped a cute lion cub, who said, "Hello, I am Luki. Are you off on an adventure? Can I join you?" Wiley and Hanifah gladly welcomed the lion cub.

All of a sudden, they noticed that the jackals had returned, with what seemed like an army of others. Luki stood in front of Wiley and Hanifah, ready to fight them bravely. Luki let out a deafening roar, which seemed to come from a much bigger lion. The jackals were terrified and scurried away. Wiley, Hanifah and brave Luki gave a sigh of relief and continued on their way.

The African heat beat down on the three friends and they were starting to lose hope. But then they saw a giant giraffe grazing on a tree. They called out to her and she brought her long neck down to their level so that they could get on. From the giraffe's neck they could see the entire Serengeti – even the watering hole. Then, Wiley gave a burst of excitement: "Look over there! My family are at your watering hole, Hanifah. We've found them!"

They thanked the giraffe and ran all the way to the watering hole. Wiley's family were so happy to see him and told him how worried they had been. Hanifah jumped into the water and gave her mum a big hug. The wildebeest, the hippo and the lion cub became the best of friends.

ACKNOWLEDGEMENTS

The authors and publishers are grateful to the following copyright holders for their permission to include their copyright works in *Collins Primary Music: Early Years Foundation Stage*.

Songs and chants

Colours shining, Dinosaur parade, Dressing up, Living in the city, Midnight, Presents for the elves, Recycled robot, Sea creatures, Snowflakes fall, Space hopper take me to Mars and **Sunflower seeds** – all traditional melodies with lyrics by Sue Nicholls © 2021 HarperCollins*Publishers* Ltd.

Being someone new, Crazy city, Growing up!, Jack Frost's fingers, Let's recycle!, Look out for rainbows, One pair of shoes, Rocket ride, The sea is stuck in a shell, The shoemaker's piggy bank and **Tyrannosaurus rex** – all by Sue Nicholls © 2021 HarperCollins*Publishers* Ltd.

Yummy, yummy yum cha and **Noodle song** – by Kathryn Wong with conceptual direction by Anders Nelsson © 2021 HarperCollins*Publishers* Ltd.

Mangwane mpulele – traditional, arranged by Otto Gumaelius © 2021 HarperCollins*Publishers* Ltd.

Come to the Serengeti by Ava Joseph © 2021 HarperCollins*Publishers* Ltd.

Stories and poems

Ai Lin cooks chow mein, Danny's tasty rainbow, My snowman, Let's find treasure, Seashells for Serena, The helpful elves, Tyro the baby dinosaur, Zigi bounces to Mars – all by Sue Nicholls © 2021 HarperCollins*Publishers* Ltd.

All aboard the pirate ship by Sue Nicholls © 2009 Sue Nicholls.

Searching in the Serengeti by Ava Joseph © 2021 HarperCollins*Publishers* Ltd.

Audio tracks

A sky full of colour, City sounds, Country sounds and **Space sounds** – all by Stephen Chadwick © 2021 HarperCollins*Publishers* Ltd.

Listening music

Listening music consultation by Helen MacGregor.

Ame no ki (Rain tree) (extract) by Toru Takemitsu, performed by Toronto New Music Ensemble. Licensed courtesy of Naxos.

Aquarium from **The carnival of the animals** by Camille Saint-Saëns, performed by Peter Toperczer, Marian Lapsansky, Slovak Radio Symphony Orchestra, Ondrej Lenard. Licensed courtesy of Naxos.

Concerto for robotic piano and strings by Stephen Chadwick © 2020 Stephen Chadwick

Dance of the knights (extract) from the **Romeo and Juliet suite** by Sergei Prokofiev, performed by Ukraine National Symphony Orchestra, Andrew Mogrelia. Licensed courtesy of Naxos.

Galop from **The comedians** by Dmitry Kabalevsky performed by Moscow Symphony Orchestra, Vasily Jelvakov. Licensed courtesy of Naxos.

Impressions: III. To the point (extract) by Jennifer Higdon, performed by Cypress String Quartet. Licensed courtesy of Naxos.

La campanella from **Grandes études de Paganini** (extract) by Franz Liszt, performed by Jenő Jandó. Licensed courtesy of Naxos.

Music of the starry night (extract) from **Music for a summer evening (Makrokosmos III)** by George Crumb, performed by Ingrid Lindgren, Barbro Dahlman, Seppo Asikainen, Rainer Kuisma. Licensed courtesy of BIS records.

Images

Cover image: Elena Schweitzer/Shutterstock; **Amazing African animals image:** Susan Schmitz/Shutterstock; **A sky full of colour image:** Troy Page Films/Shutterstock; **A tale from long ago image:** Shaiith/Shutterstock; **Beyond the stars image:** lem/Shutterstock; **Busy city image:** IR Stone/Shutterstock; **Do you see dinosaurs? image:** iurii/Shutterstock; **Fabulous food image:** Indian Food Images/Shutterstock; **Let's go green! image:** Rawpixel.com/Shutterstock; **London bus:** Lebedev Yury/Shutterstock; **Rocket:** versuche zu beten/Shutterstock; **Sunflowers in a vase:** Vavalis/Shutterstock; **Sunflowers growing:** Kalinin Ilya/Shutterstock; **Under the sea image:** Wendy Moore Photography/Shutterstock; **When snowflakes fall image:** FamVeld/Shutterstock; **Who shall I be today? image:** Dimaris/Shutterstock

Videos

A sky full of colour: Troy Page Films/Shutterstock; **Geyser video:** synthetic/Shutterstock; **Serengeti video:** BlackBoxGuild/Shutterstock

Music setting by Sarah Lofthouse, SEL Music Art Ltd.

Backing tracks created by Alan Penman.

Songs and chants performed by Louise Victoria, Baker Mukasa, Alan Penman, Kathryn Wong, Otto Gumaelius and Ava Joseph.

Stories and poems narrated by Rachael Louise Miller, Baker Mukasa and Sue Nicholls.

Sound engineering by Alan Penman, Ayo Vincent and Stephen Chadwick.

Mangwane mpulele and **Come to the Serengeti** developed in partnership with World Heart Beat Music Academy (worldheartbeat.org). Percussion: Wilf Cameron Marples; keyboards: Ayo Vincent; bass: Ezekiel Ajie; mastering: James Joseph.

Special thanks to Nikki Walters and Andy Burt from Early Excellence, Nana-Adwoa Mbeutcha from Black Mums Upfront and Annie Hickman. Your invaluable input is so appreciated.

Every effort has been made to trace and acknowledge copyright owners. If any right has been omitted, the publishers offer their apologies, and will rectify this in subsequent editions following notification.

First published 2021

Published by Collins, an imprint of HarperCollins*Publishers* Ltd
The News Building
1 London Bridge Street
London Bridge
SE1 9GF

HarperCollins*Publishers*
1st Floor Watermarque Building
Ringsend Road
Dublin 4
Ireland
www.collins.co.uk

© 2021 HarperCollins*Publishers* Ltd
10 9 8 7 6 5 4 3 2 1
ISBN: 978-0-00-844765-6

Printed and bound in Great Britain by Caligraving, Thetford, Norfolk
Designed by Fresh Lemon Australia.
Edited by Emily Wilson.

All rights reserved. No part of this publication may be reproduced or used in any form or by any means – photographic, electronic or mechanical, including photocopying, recording or information storage and retrieval systems – without the prior permission in writing of the publishers.

MIX
Paper from responsible sources
FSC C007454

This book is produced from independently certified FSC™ paper to ensure responsible forest management.

For more information visit:
www.harpercollins.co.uk/green